The Big Coloring Book of Cats

(Dedicated to the Purrrr-babies in our lives
and to those who love them!)

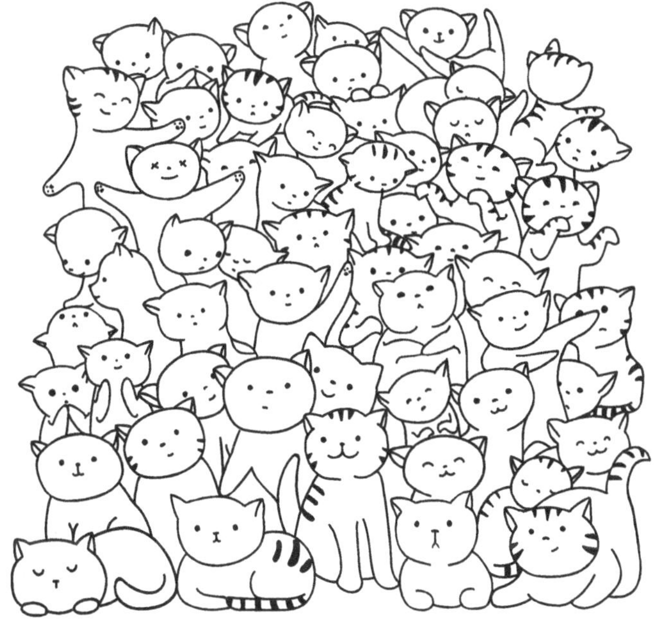

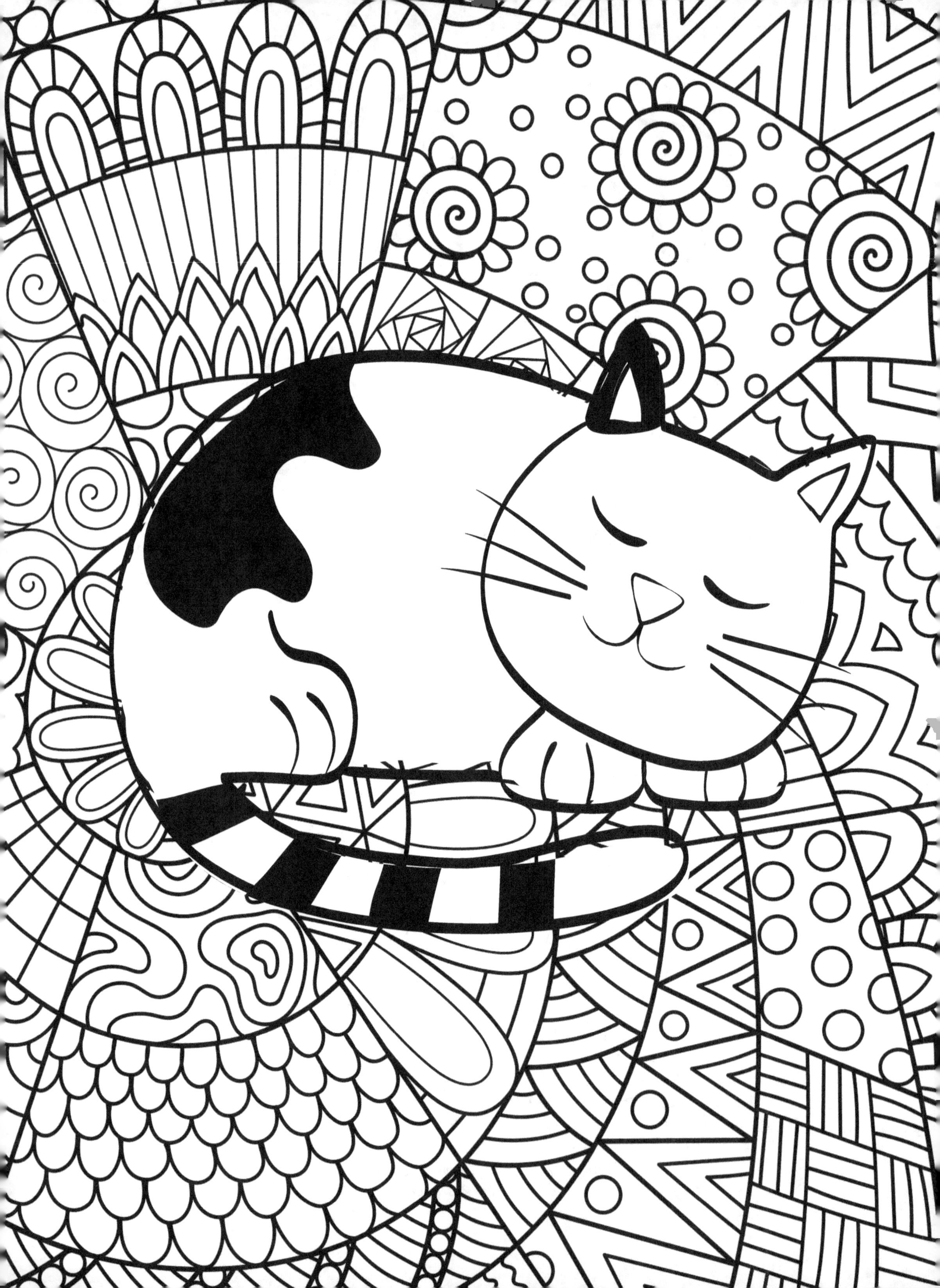

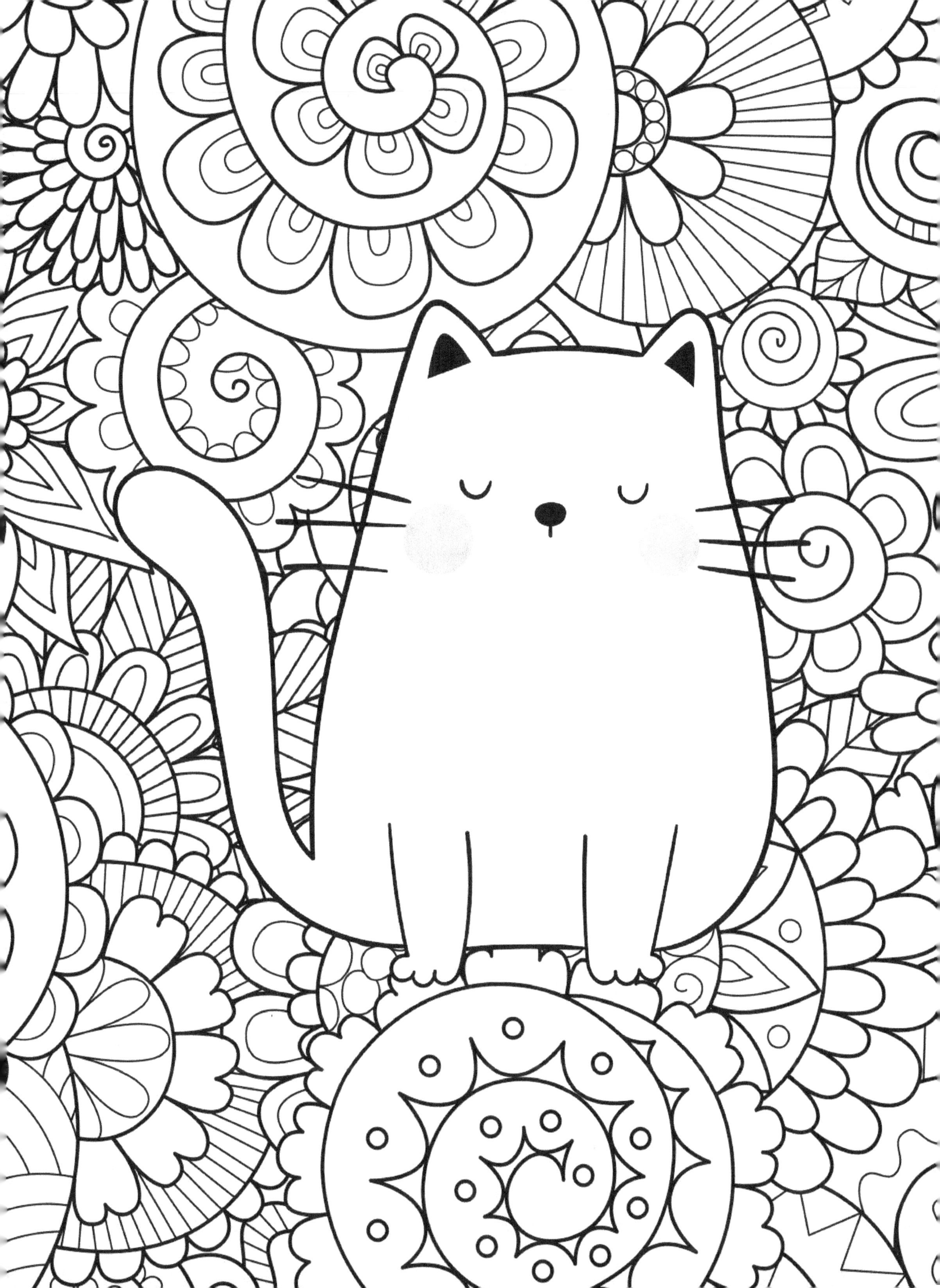

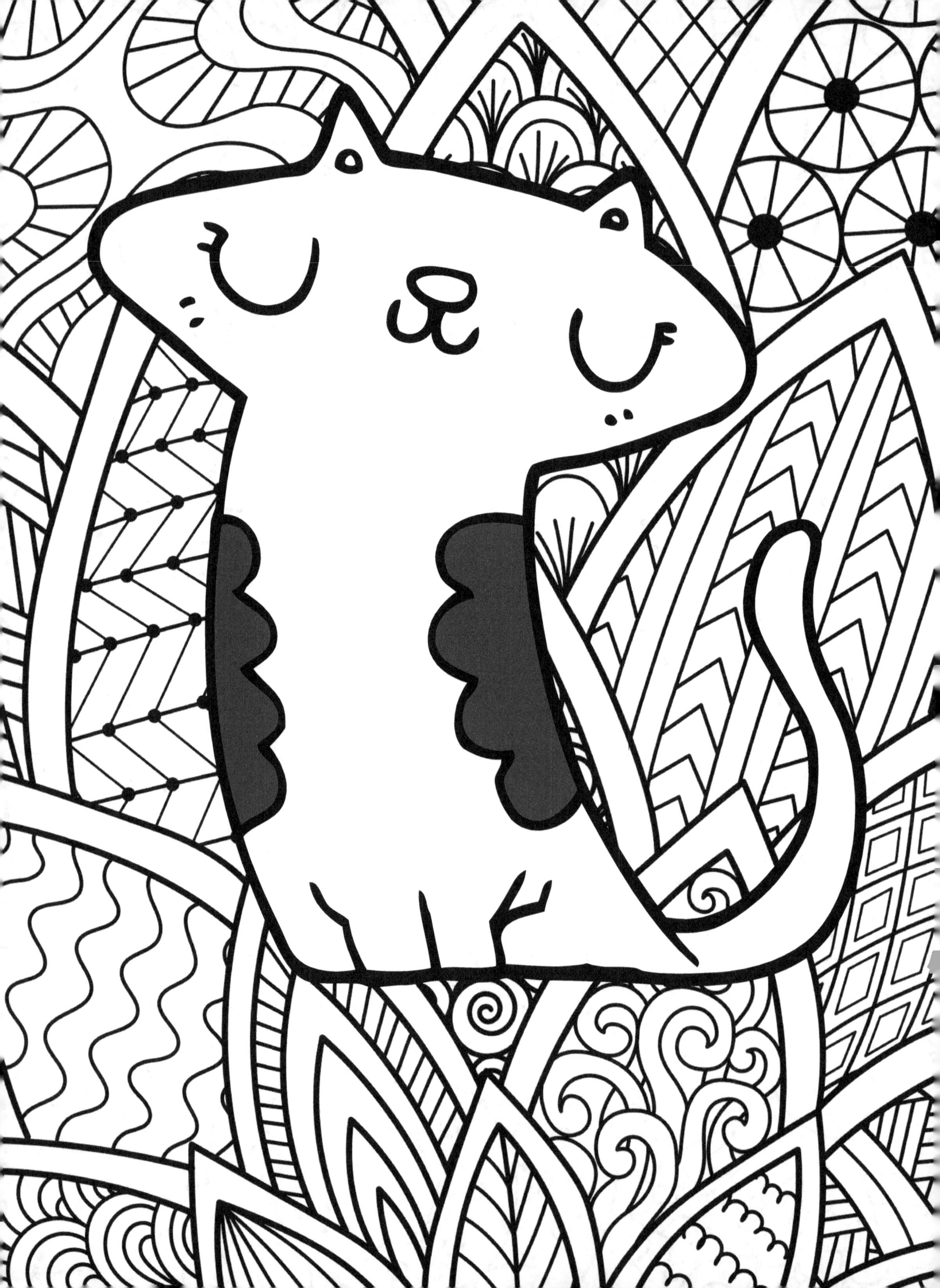

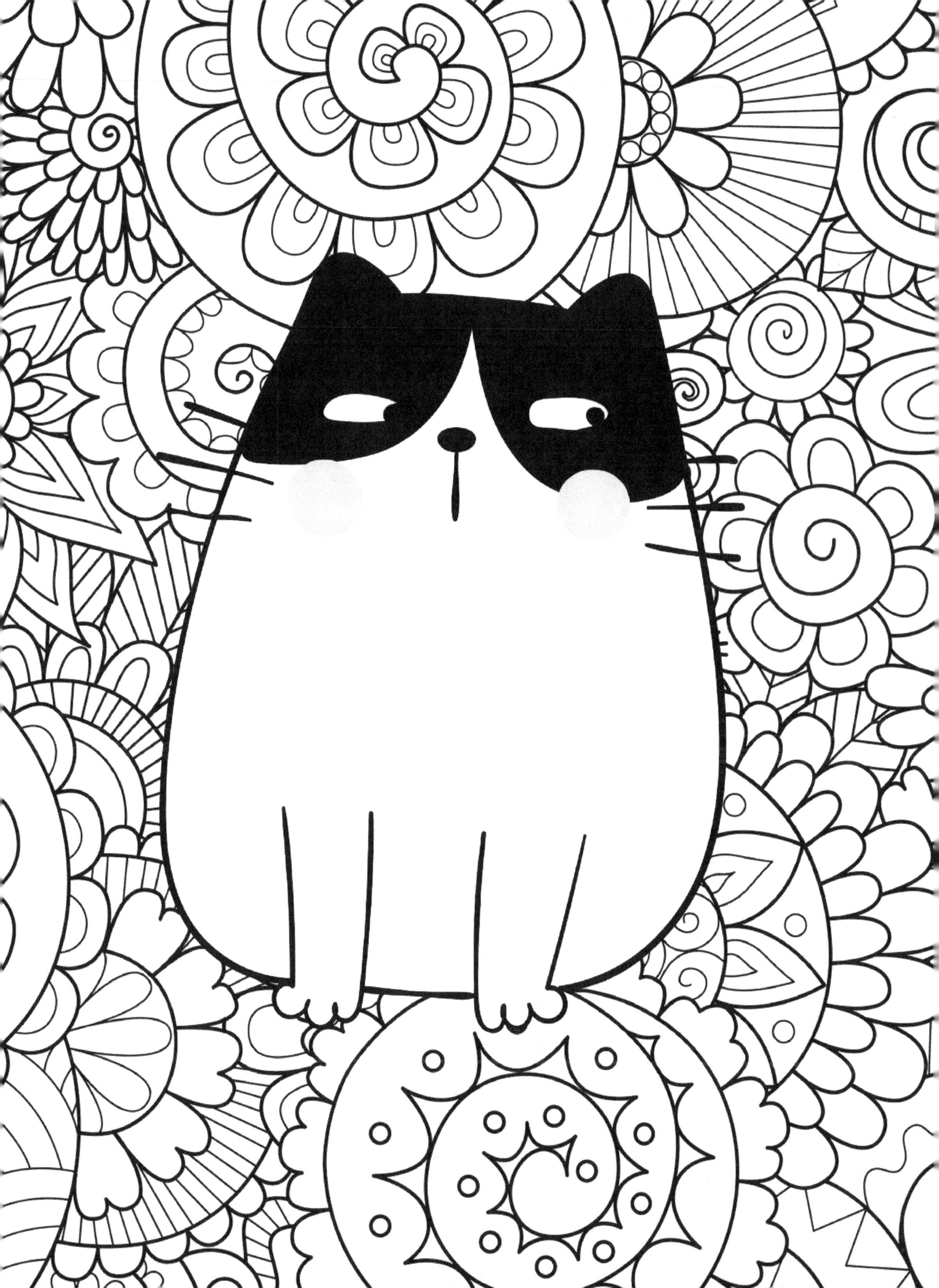

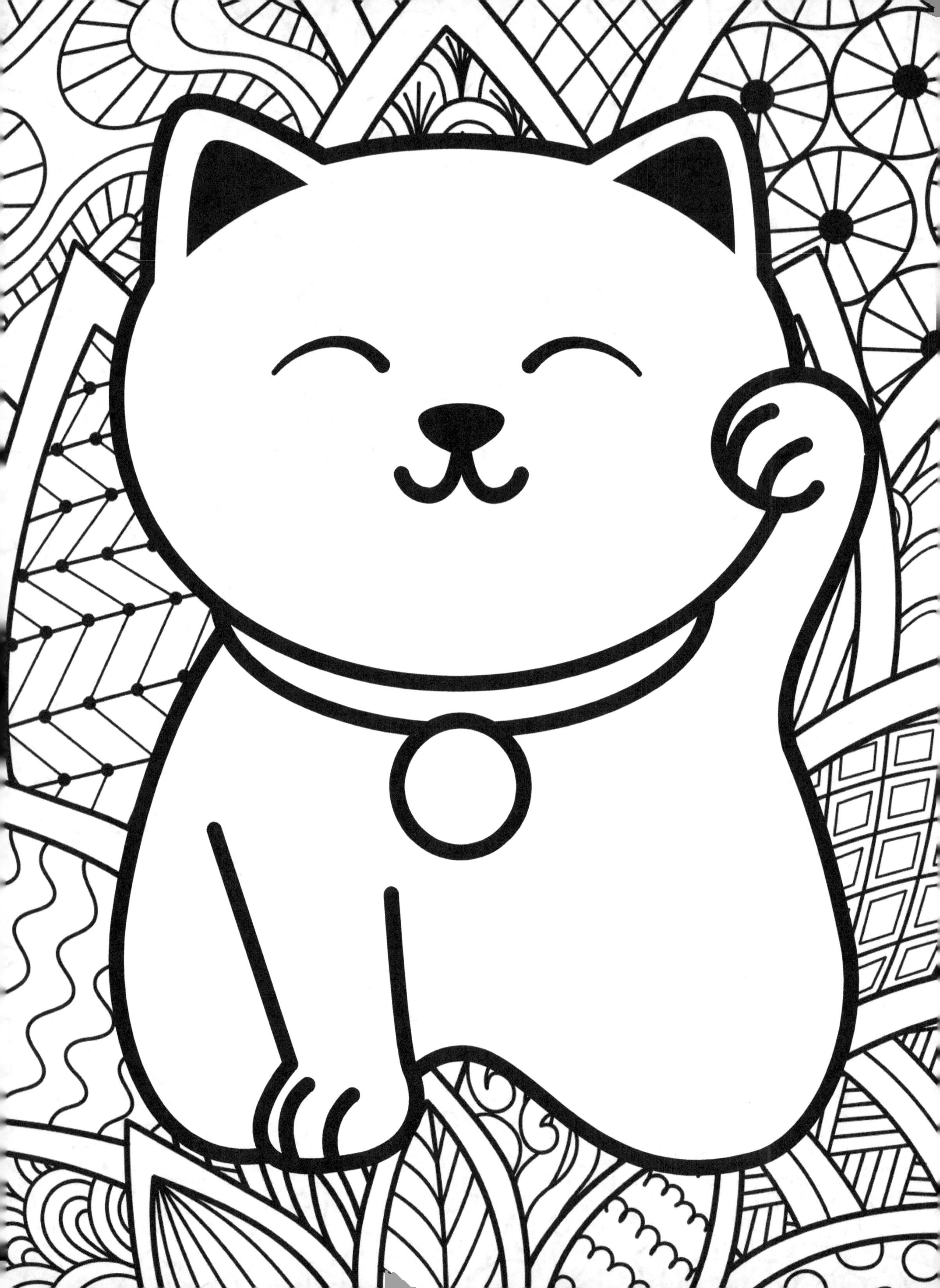

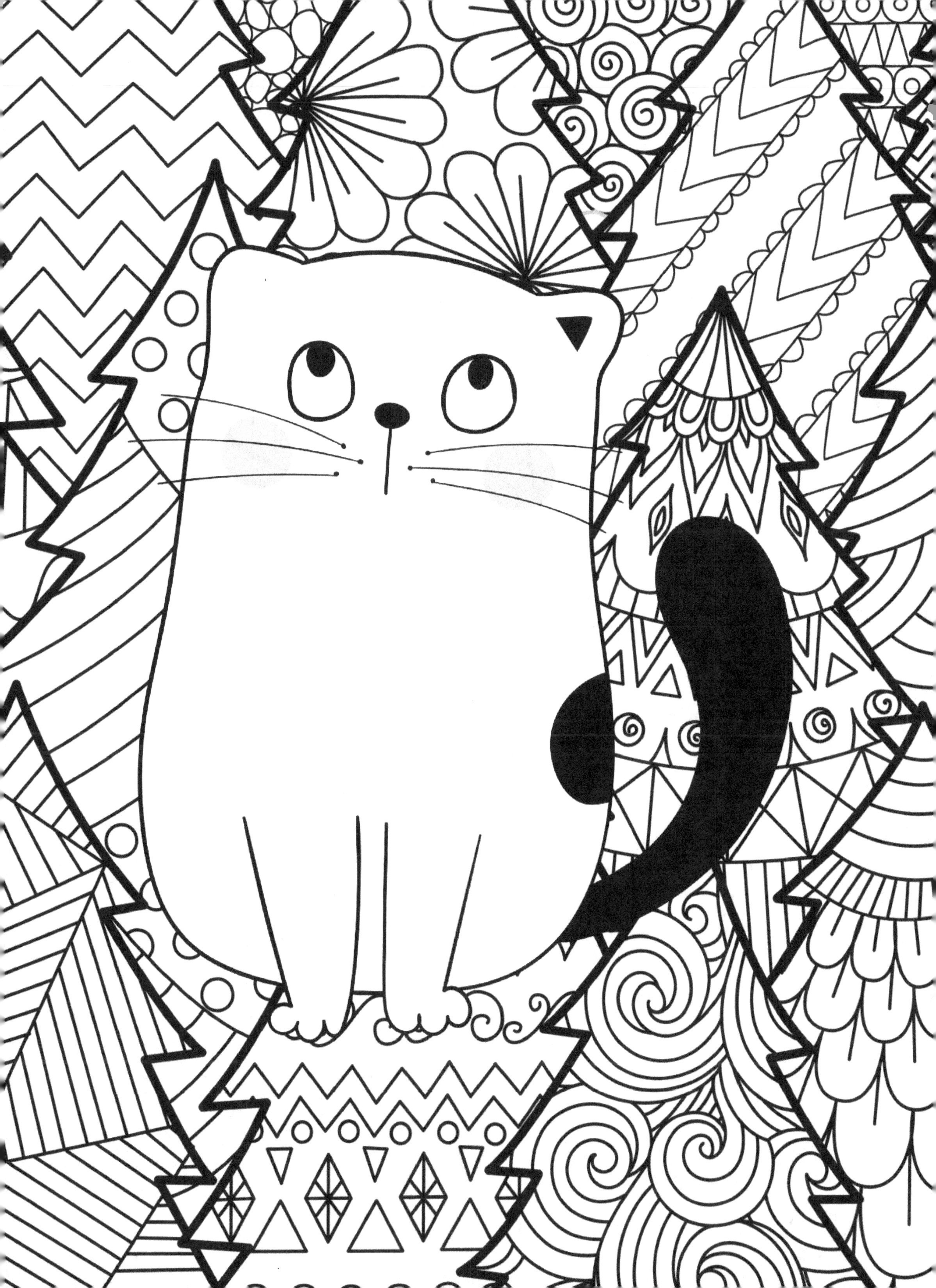

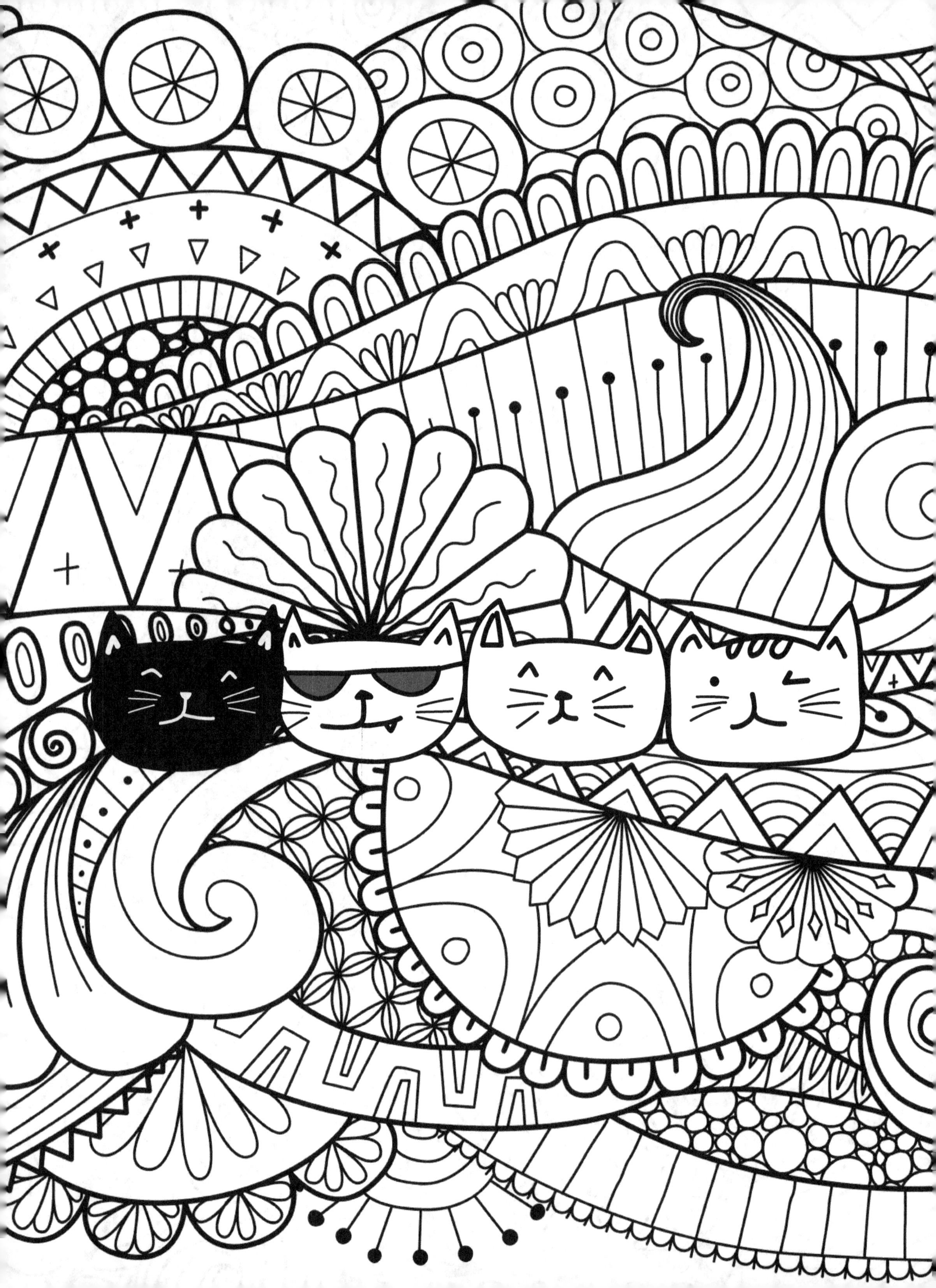

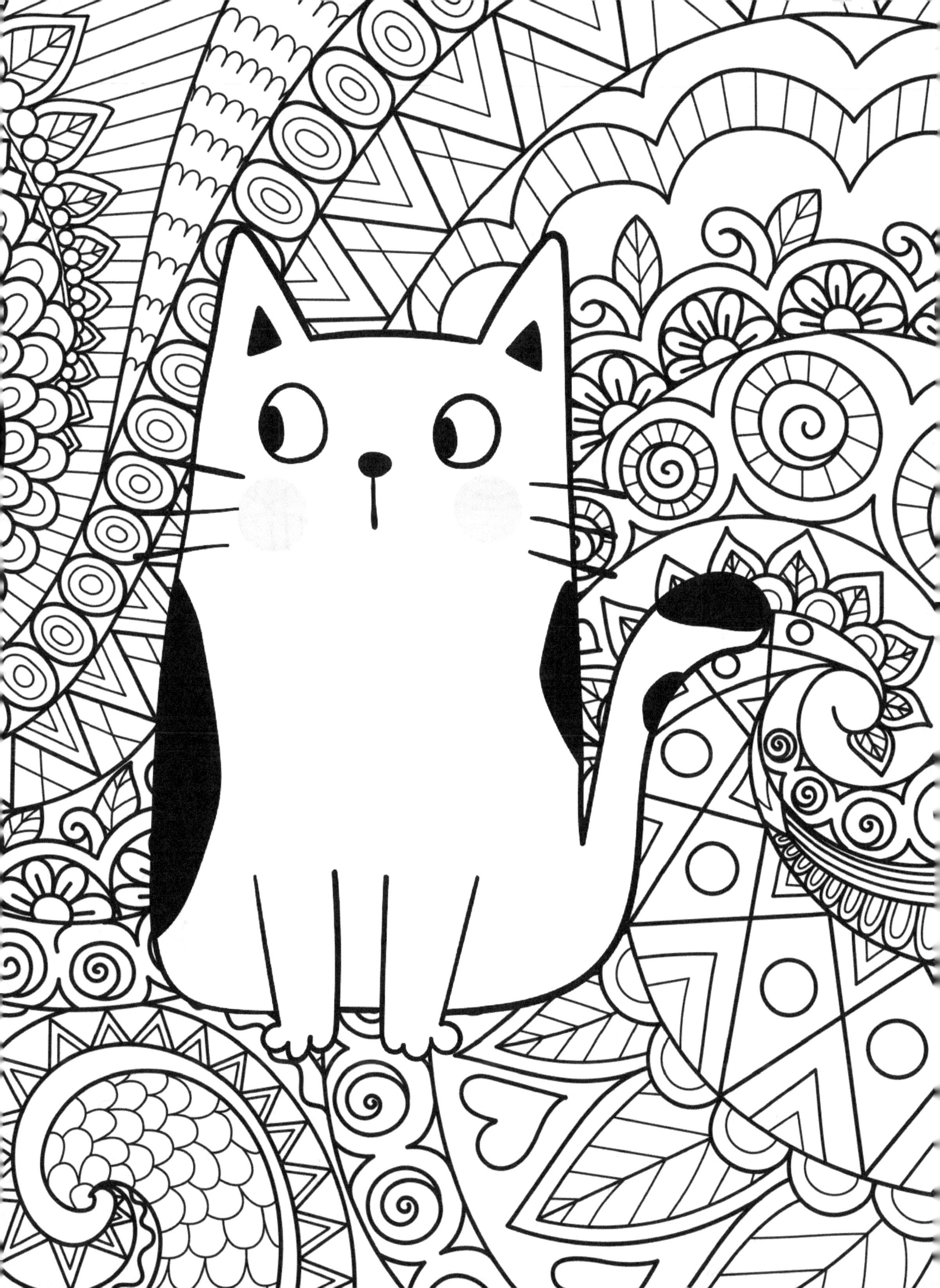

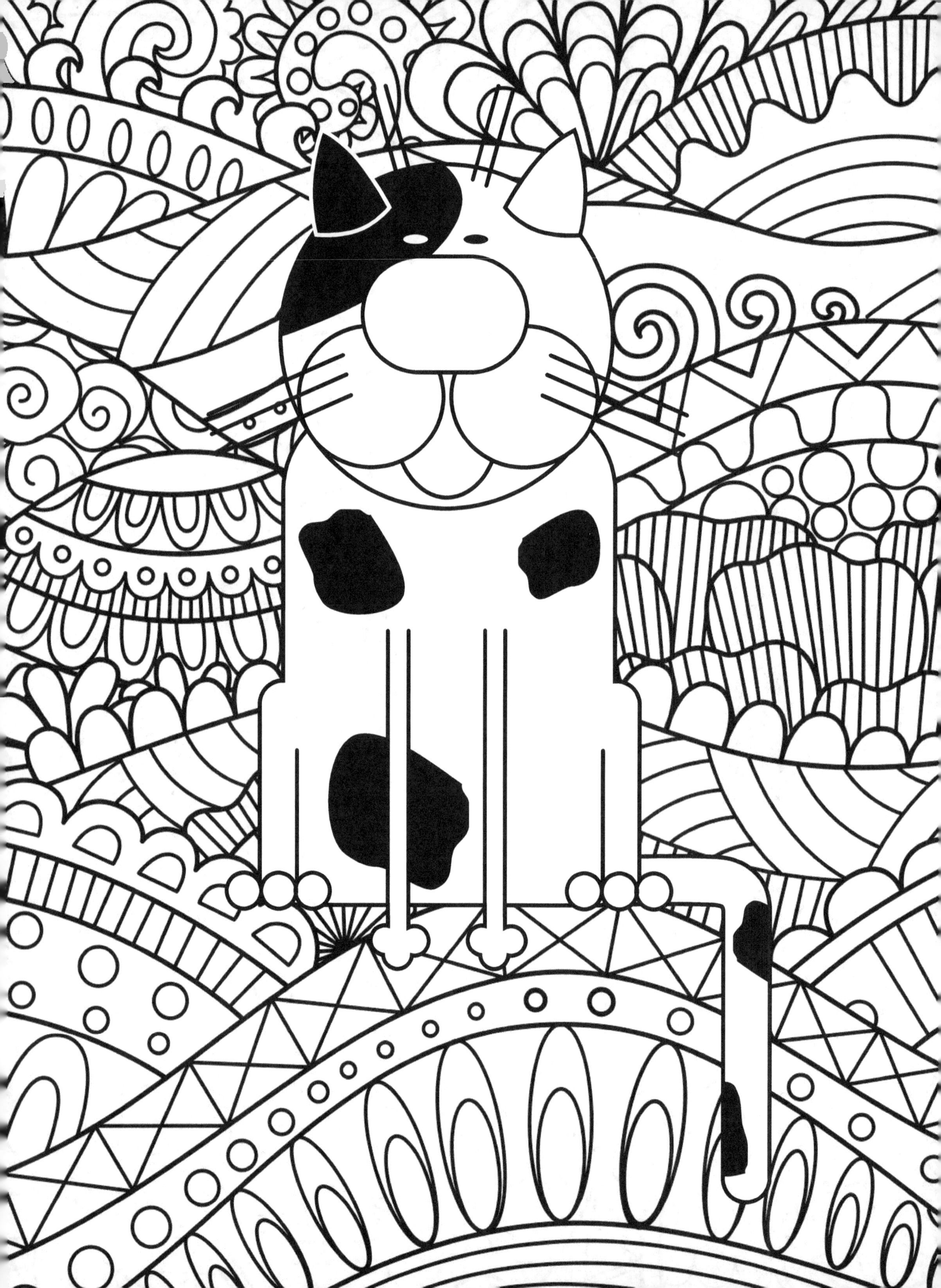

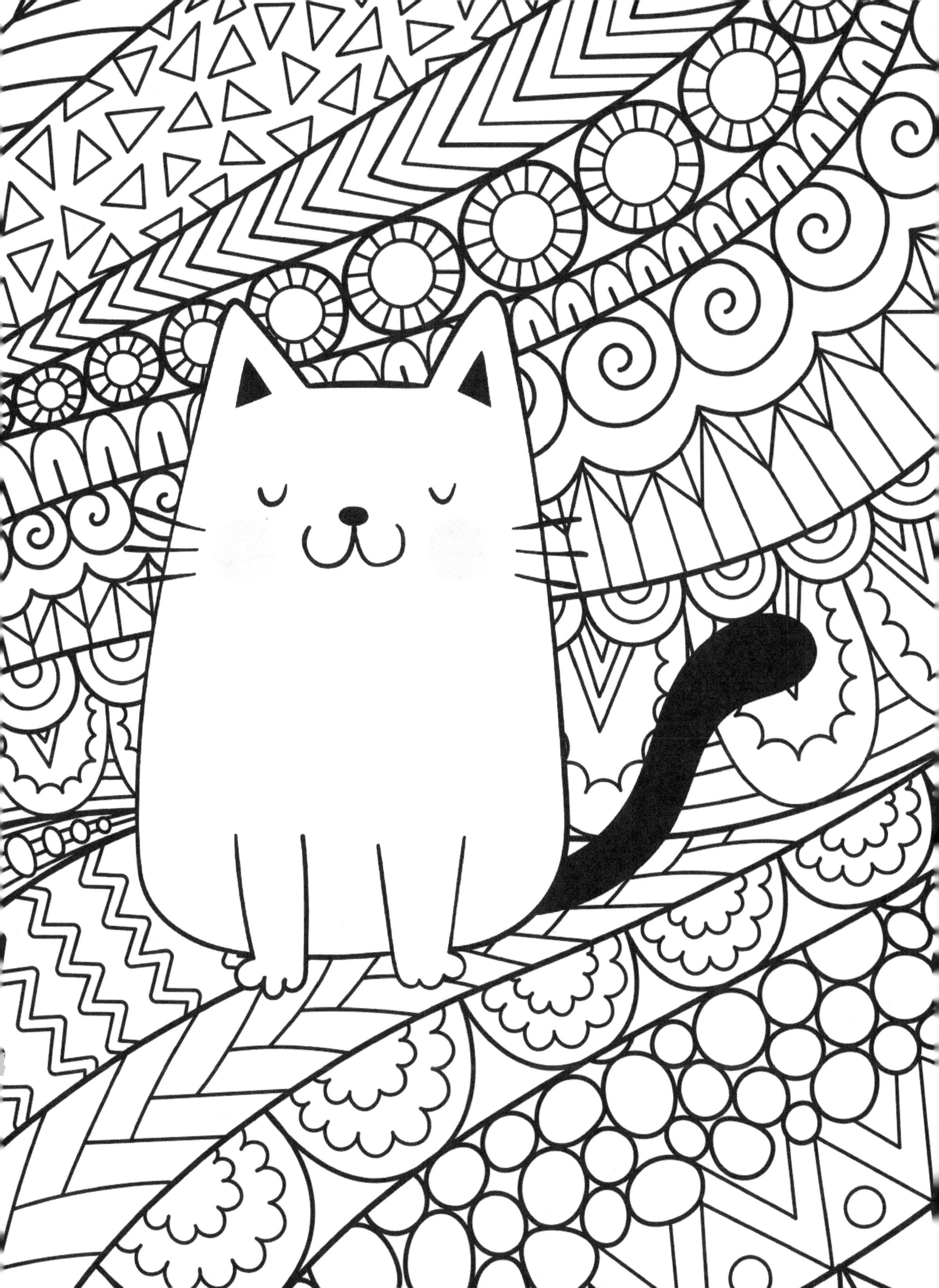

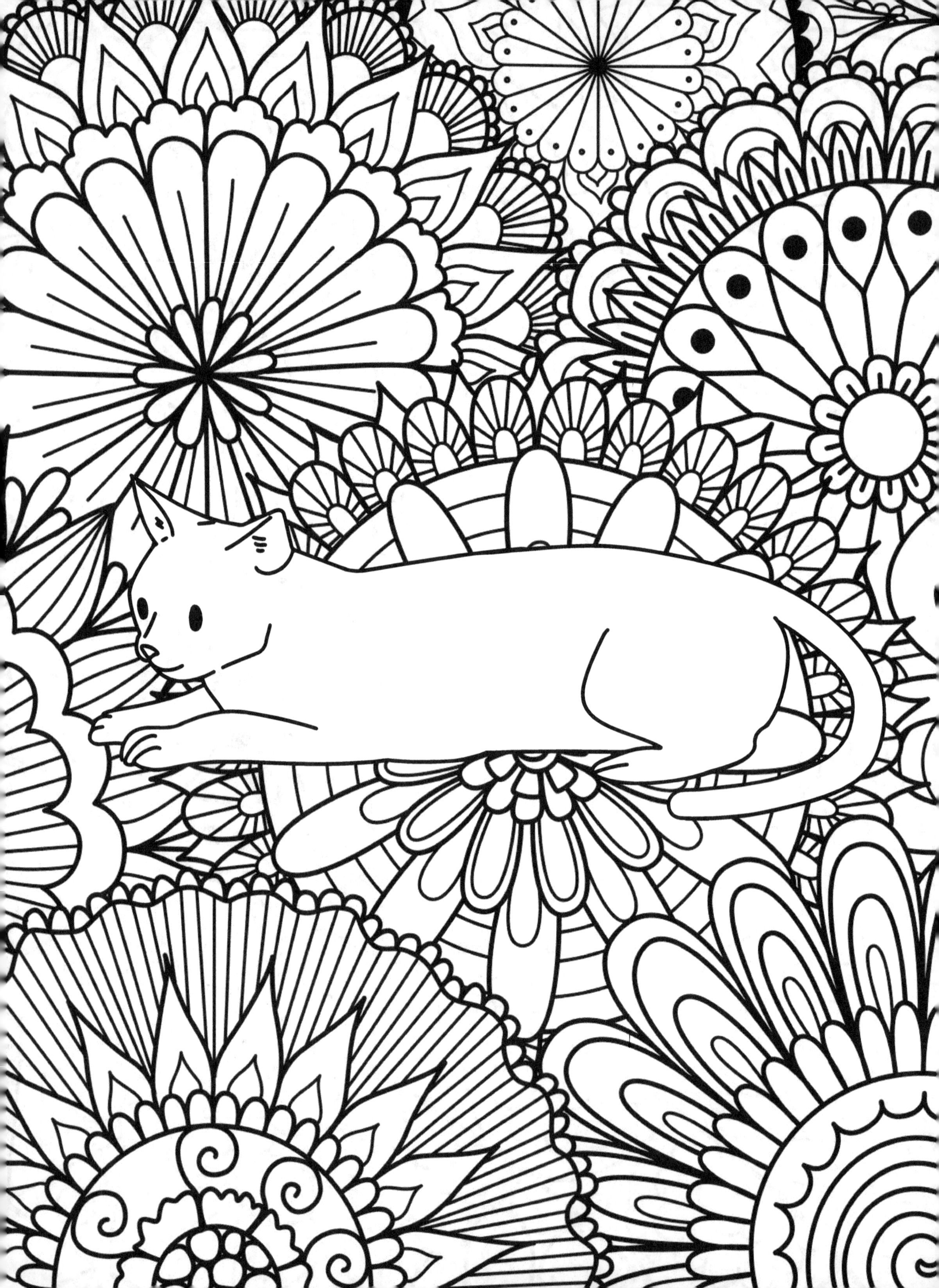

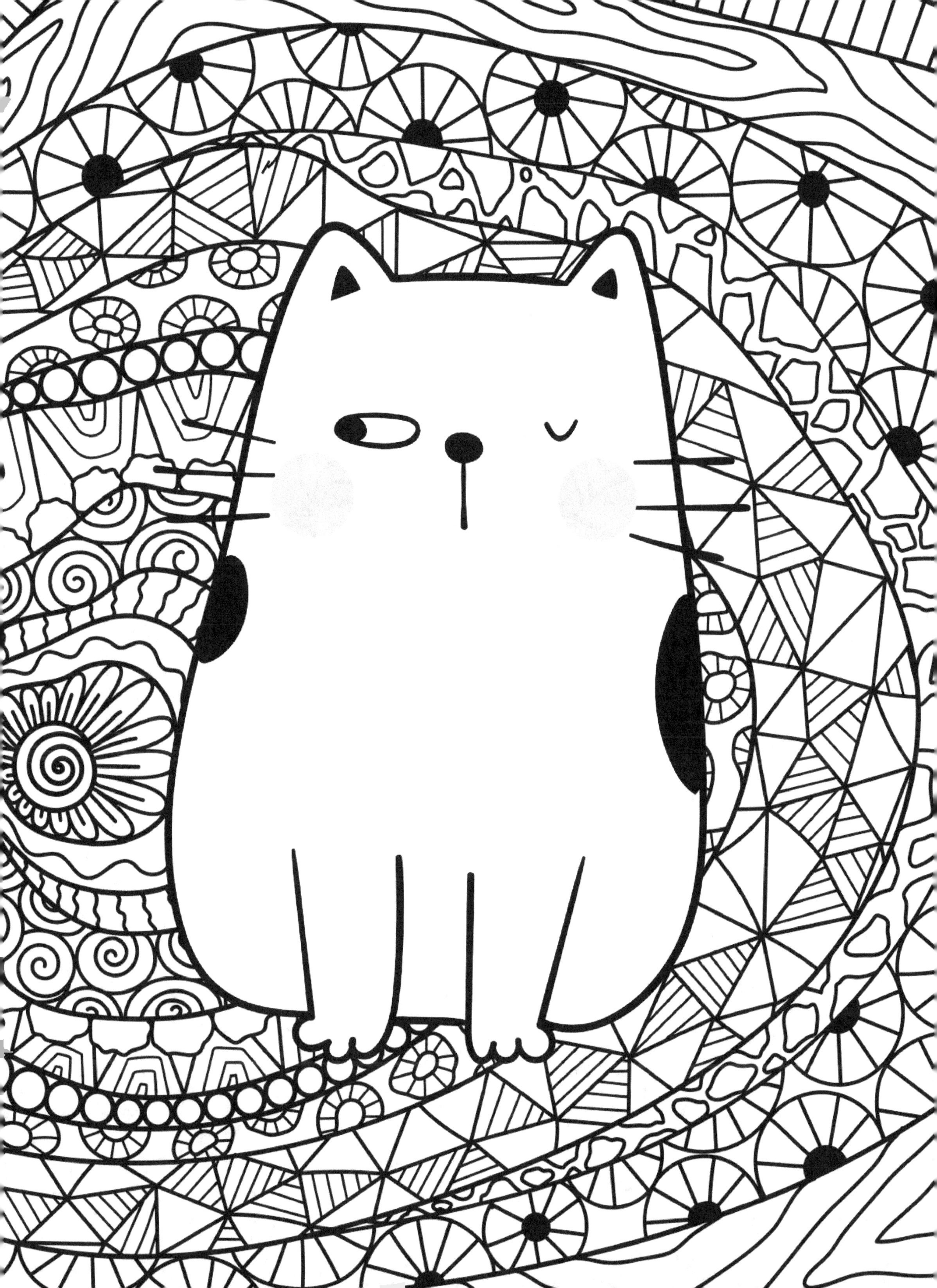

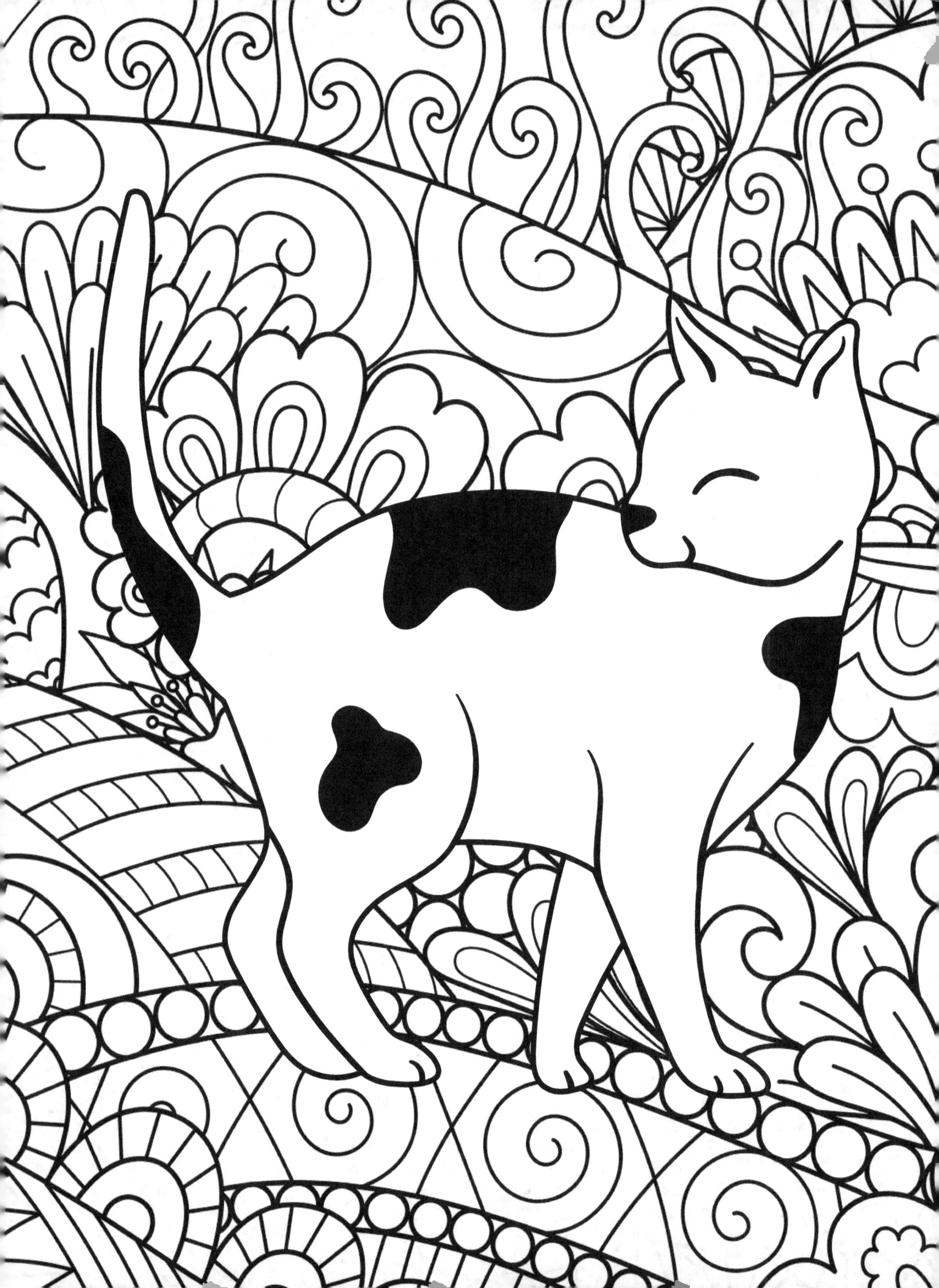

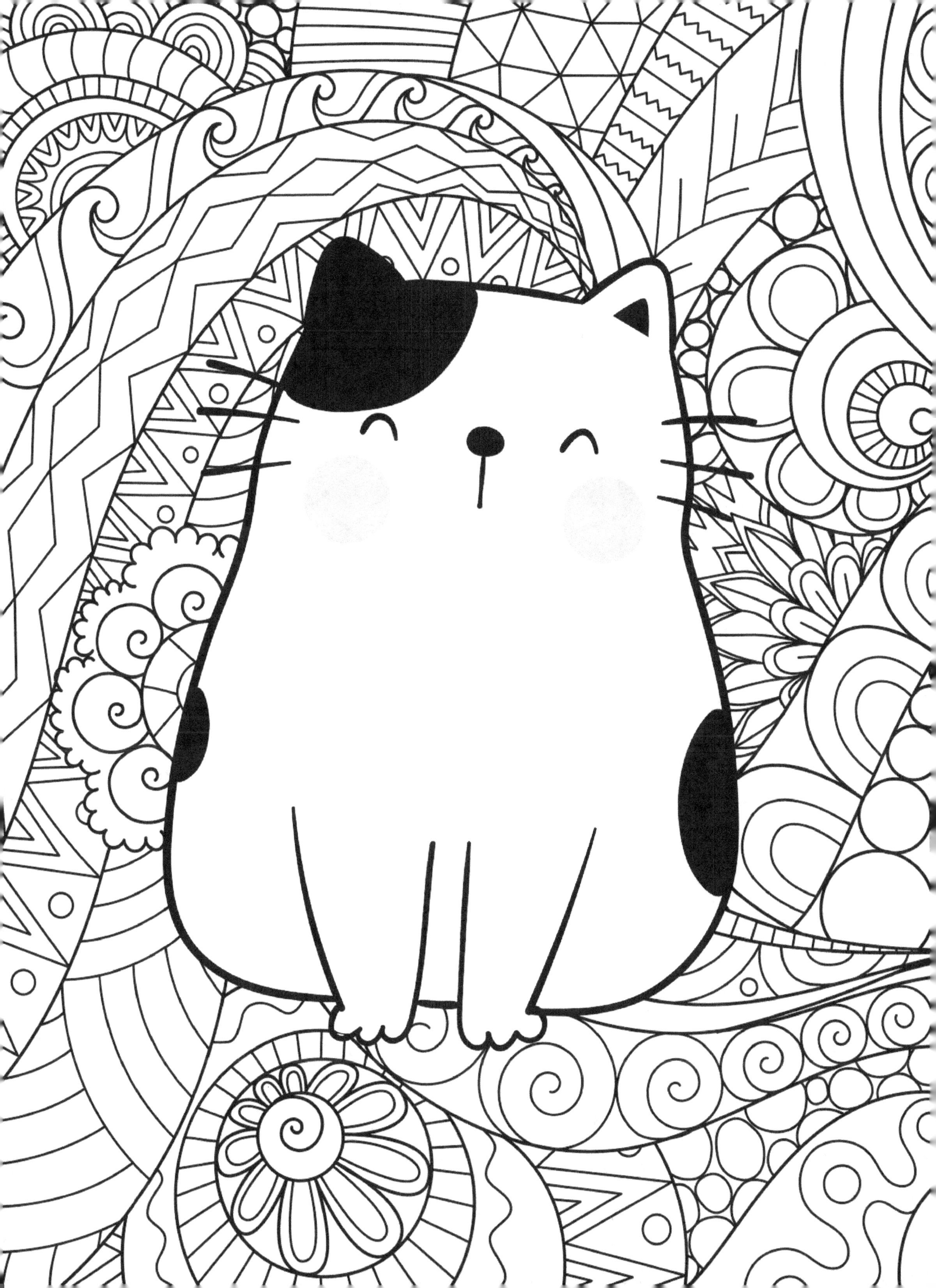

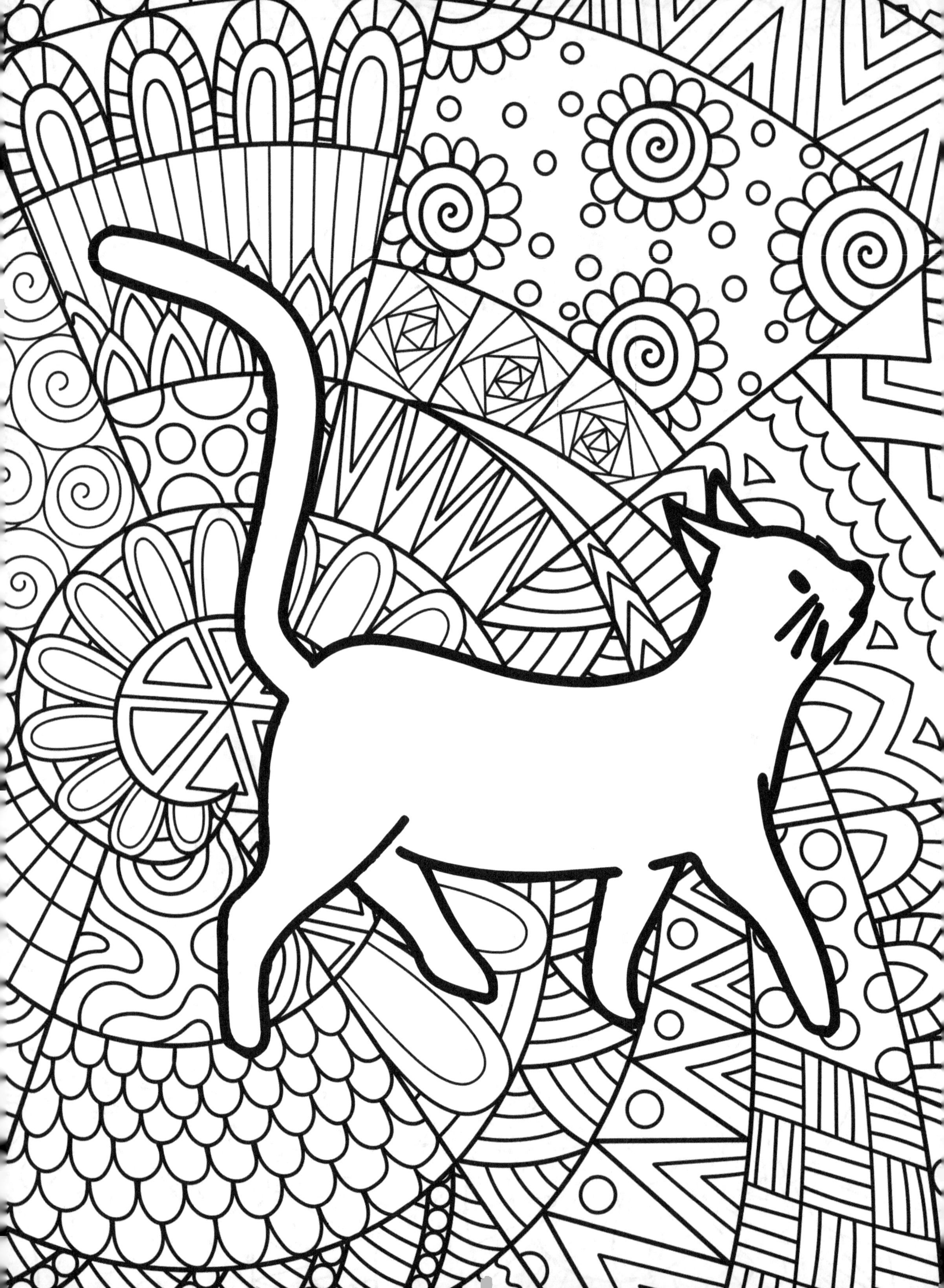

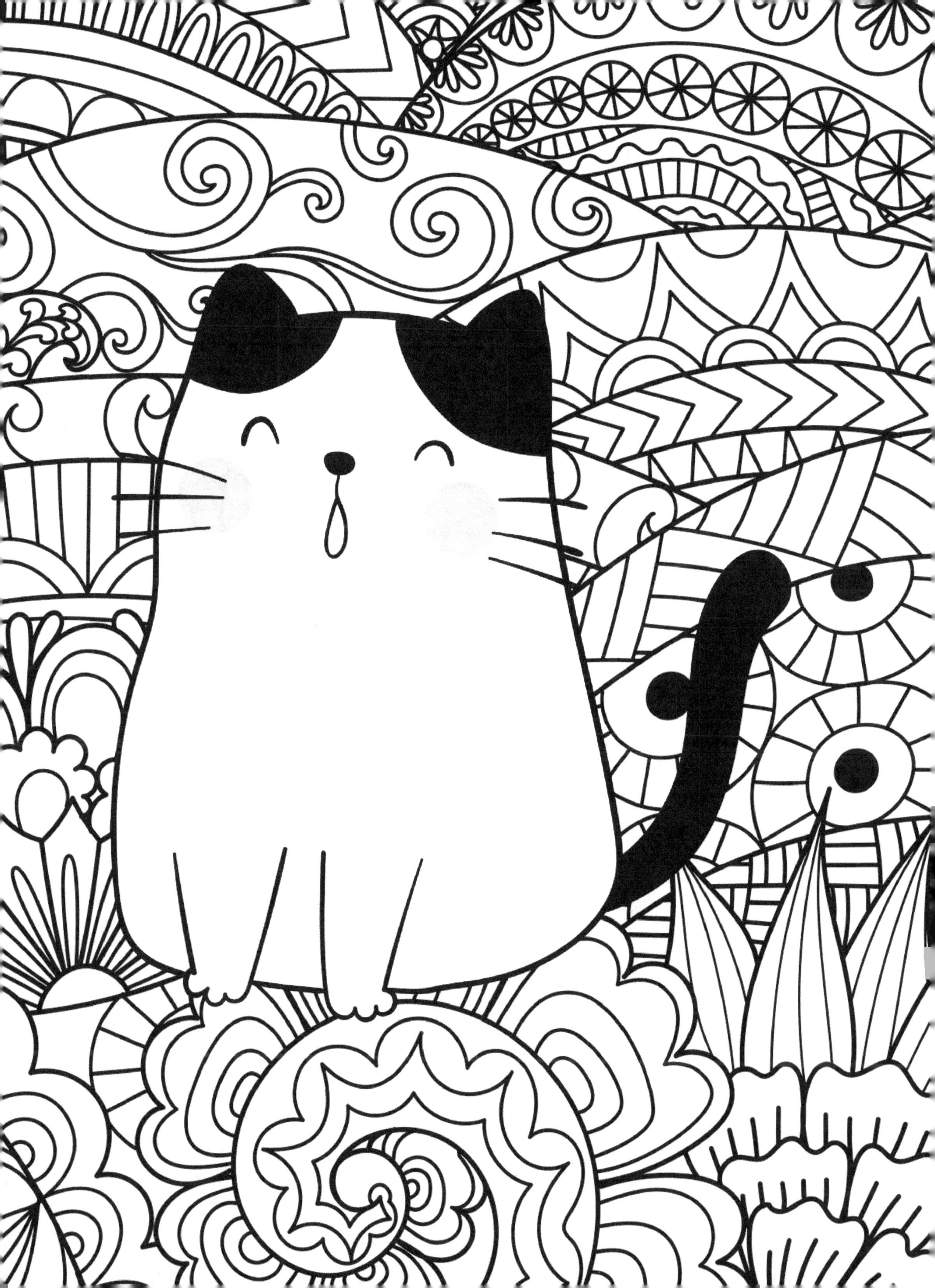

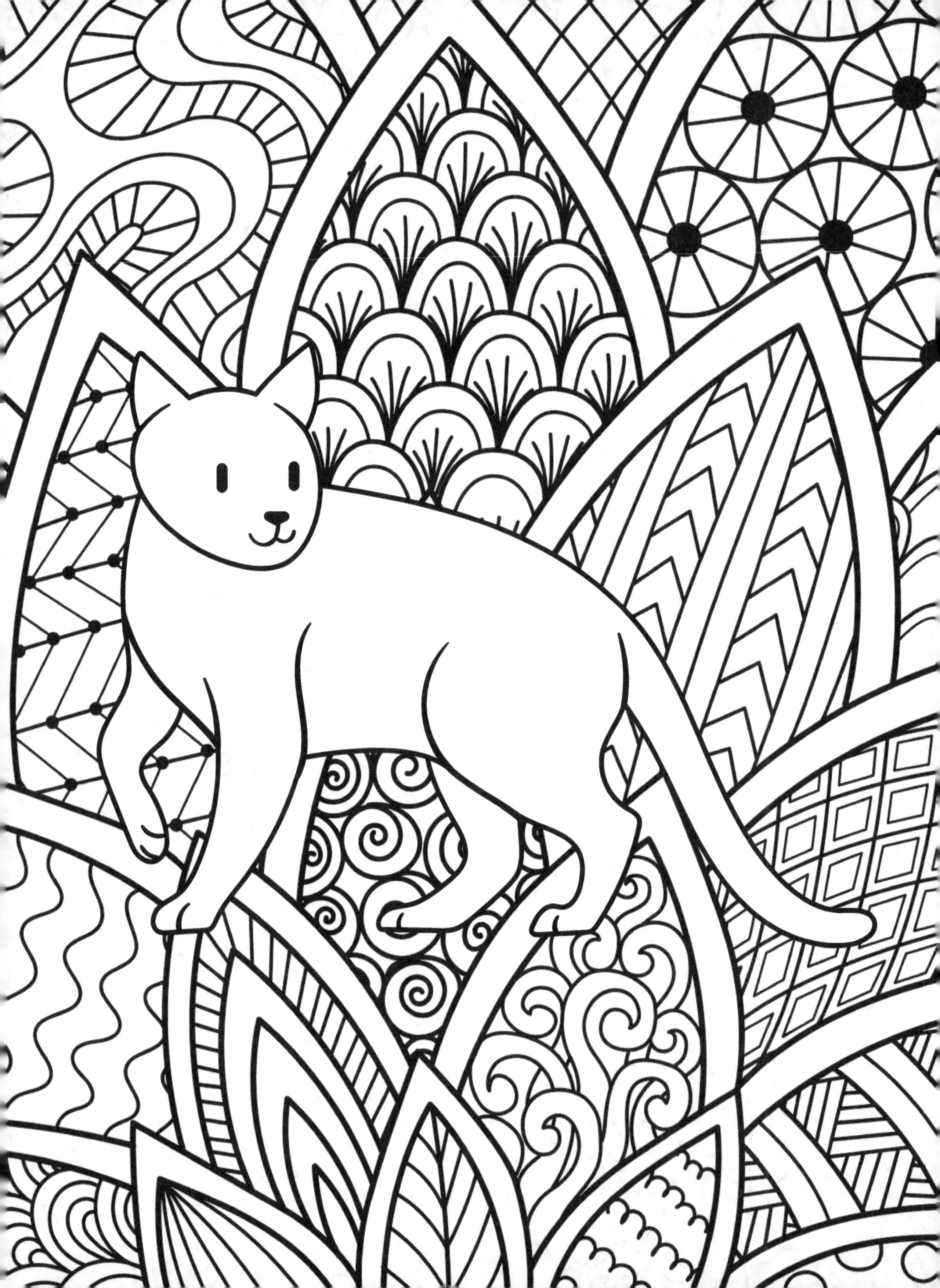

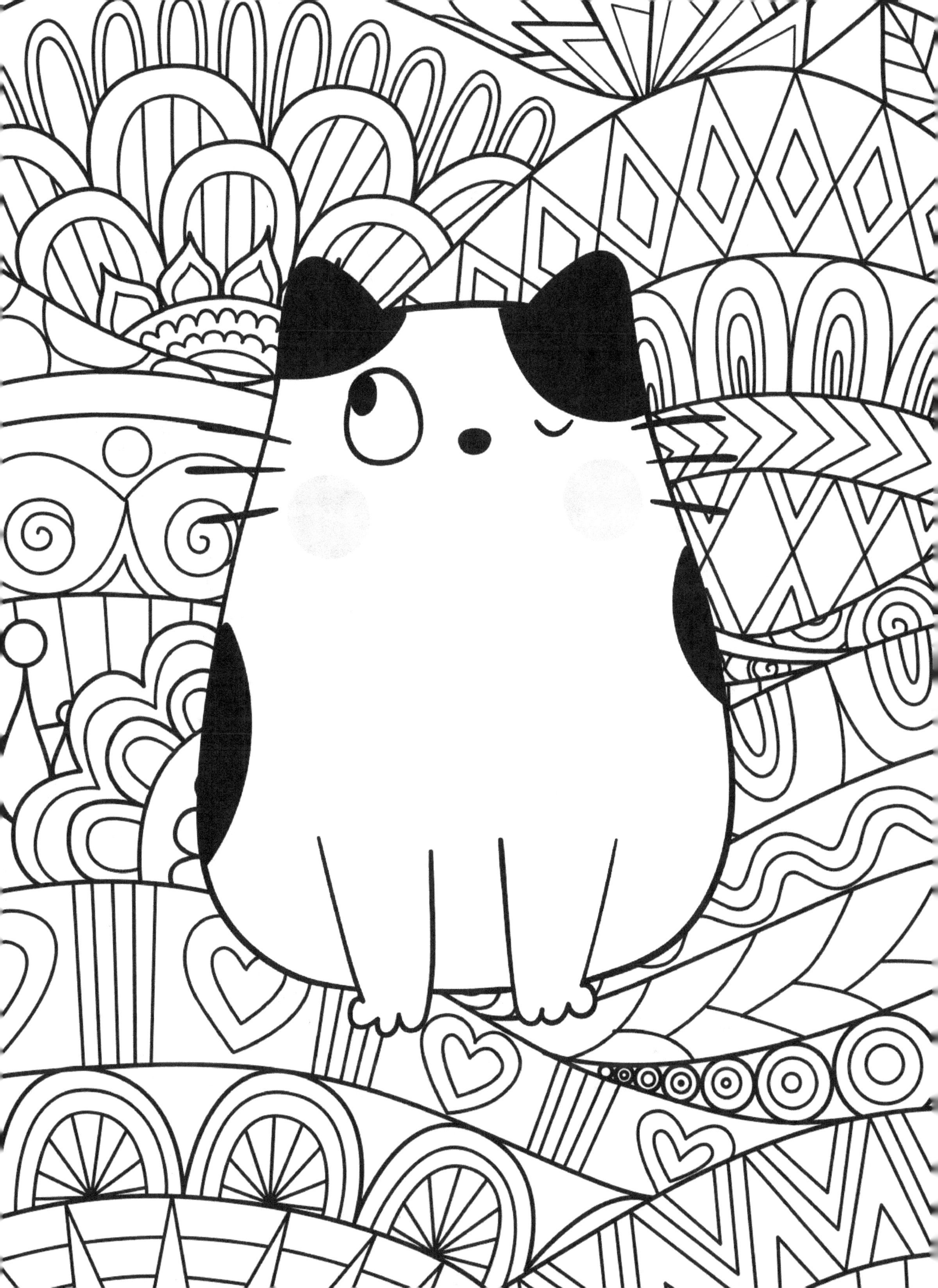

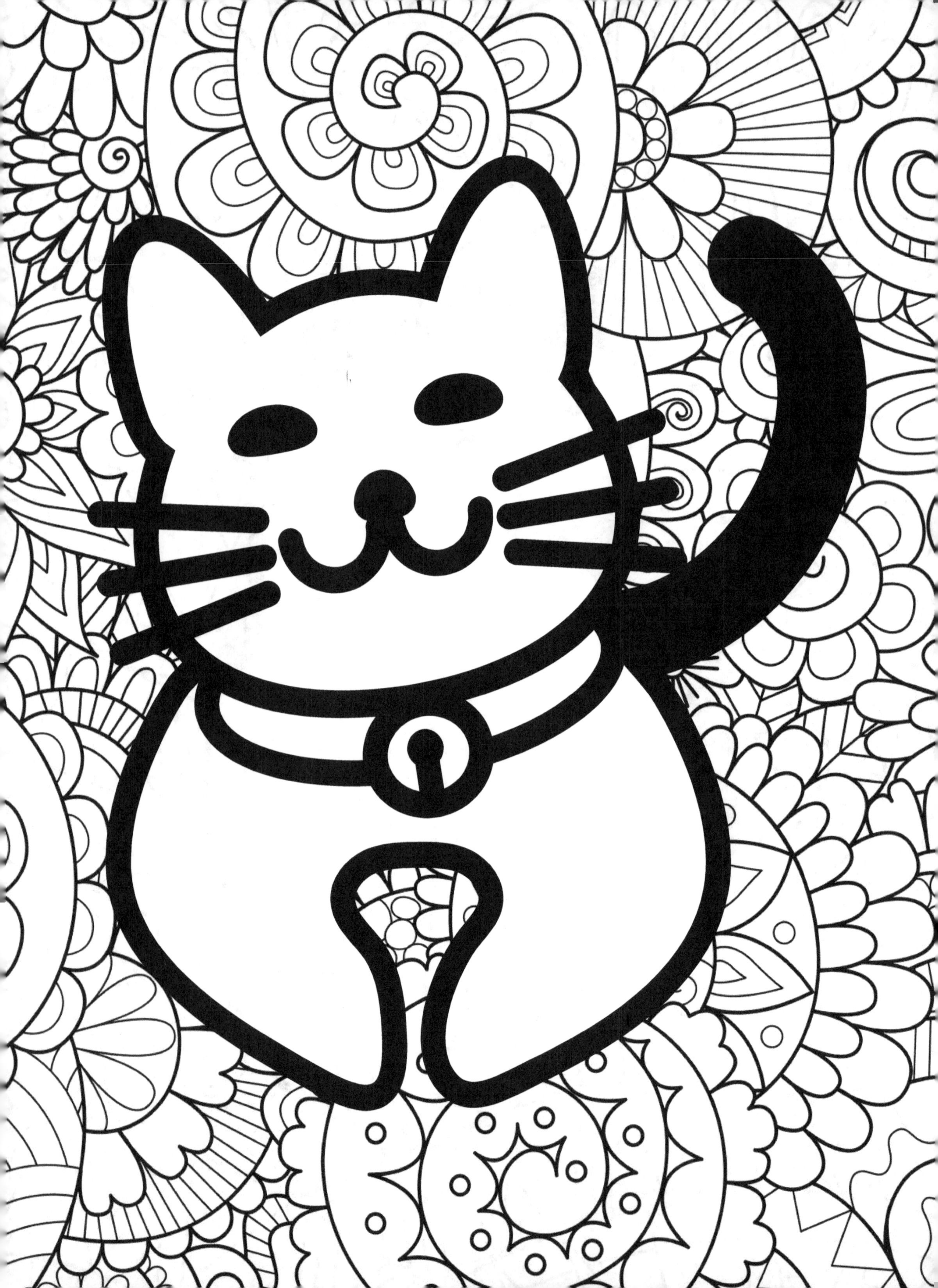

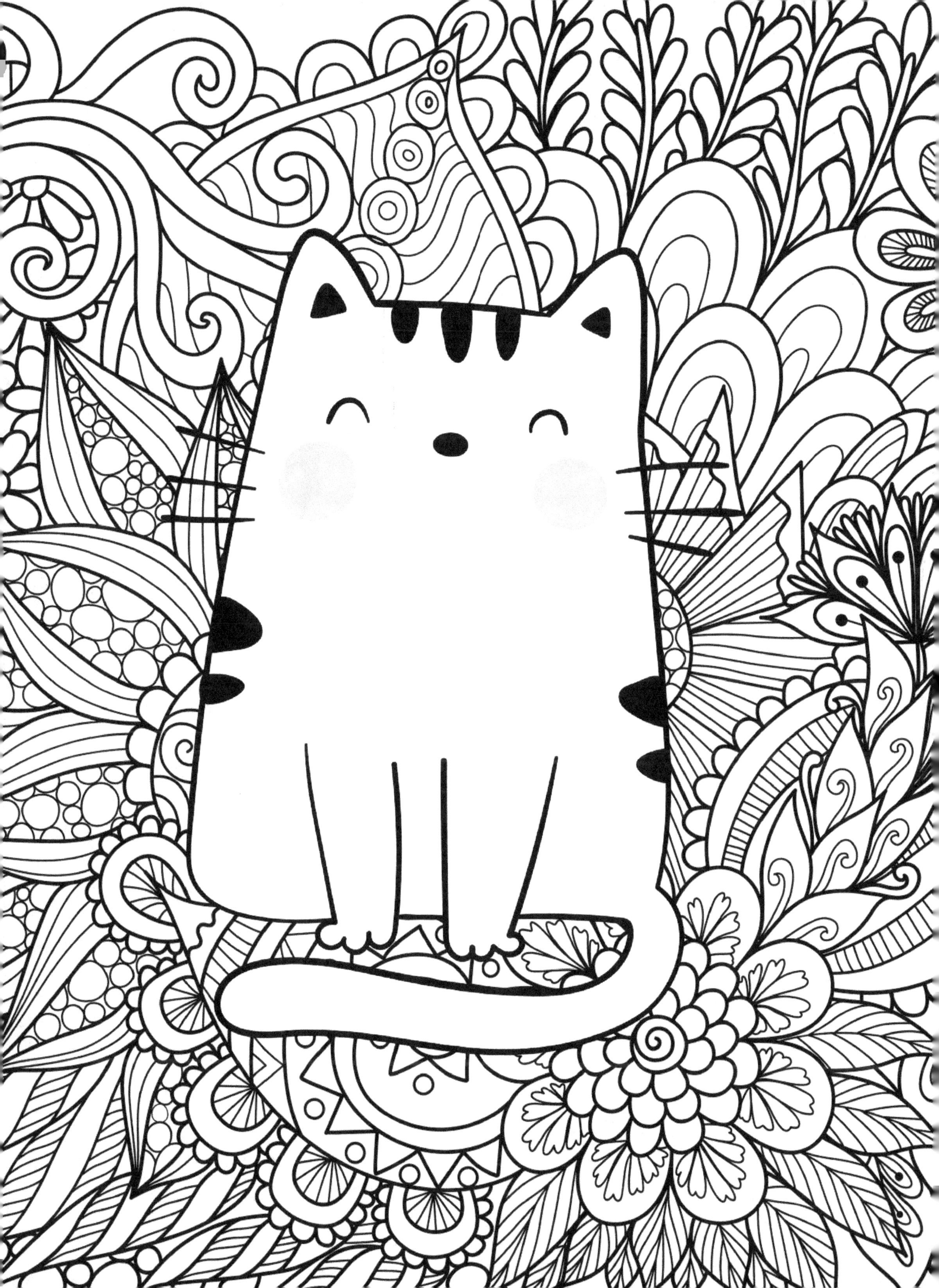

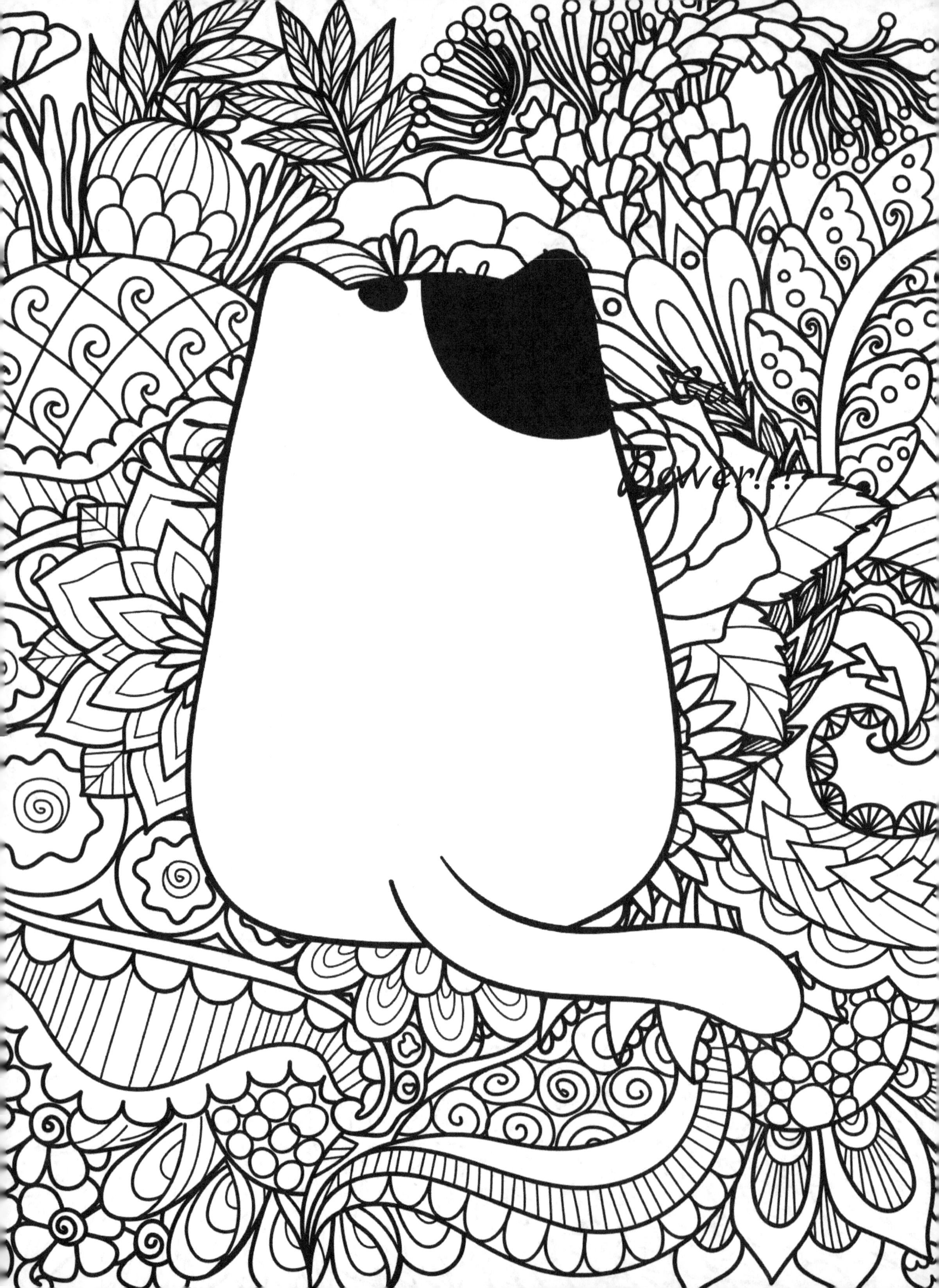
flower!...

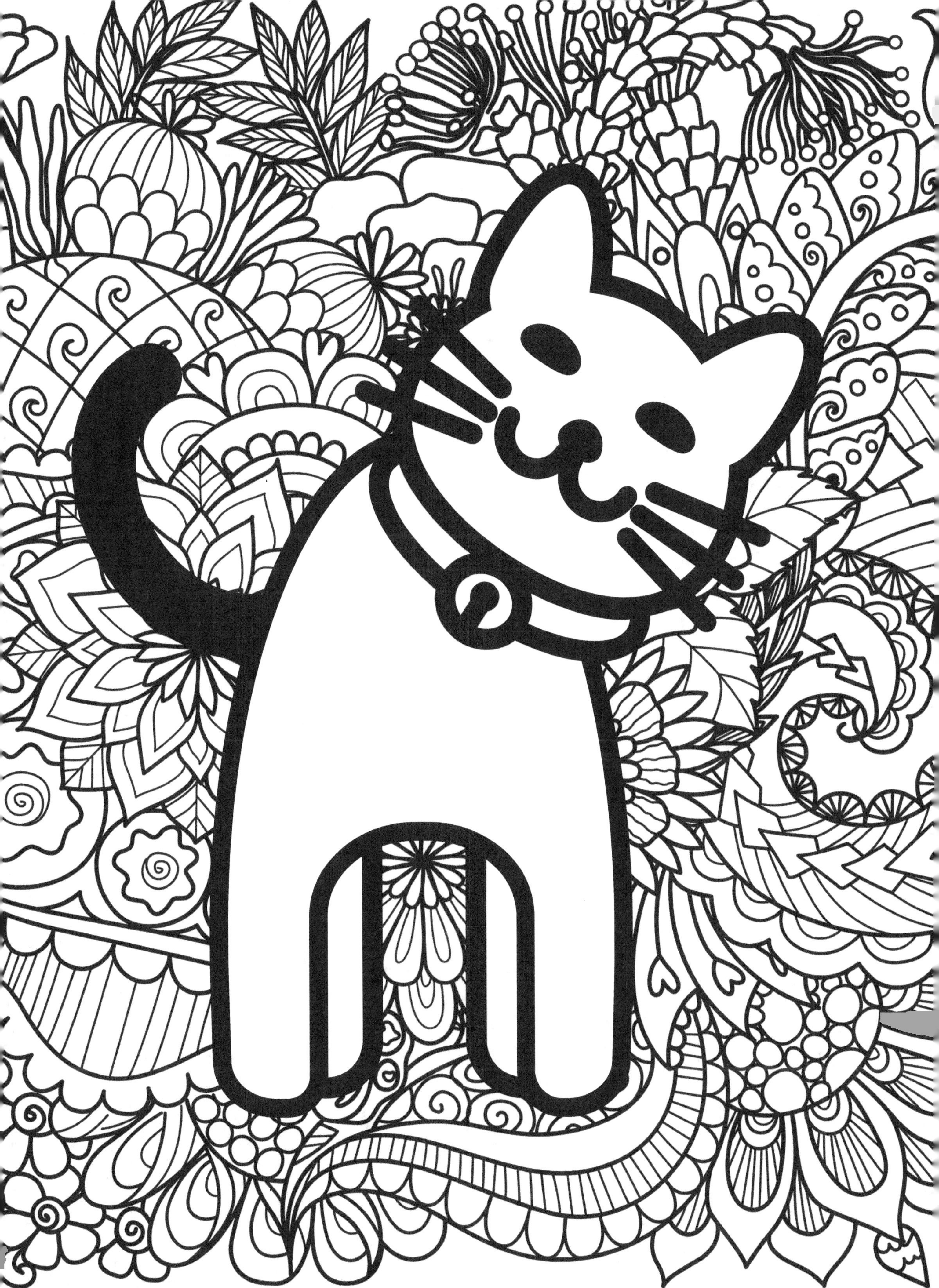

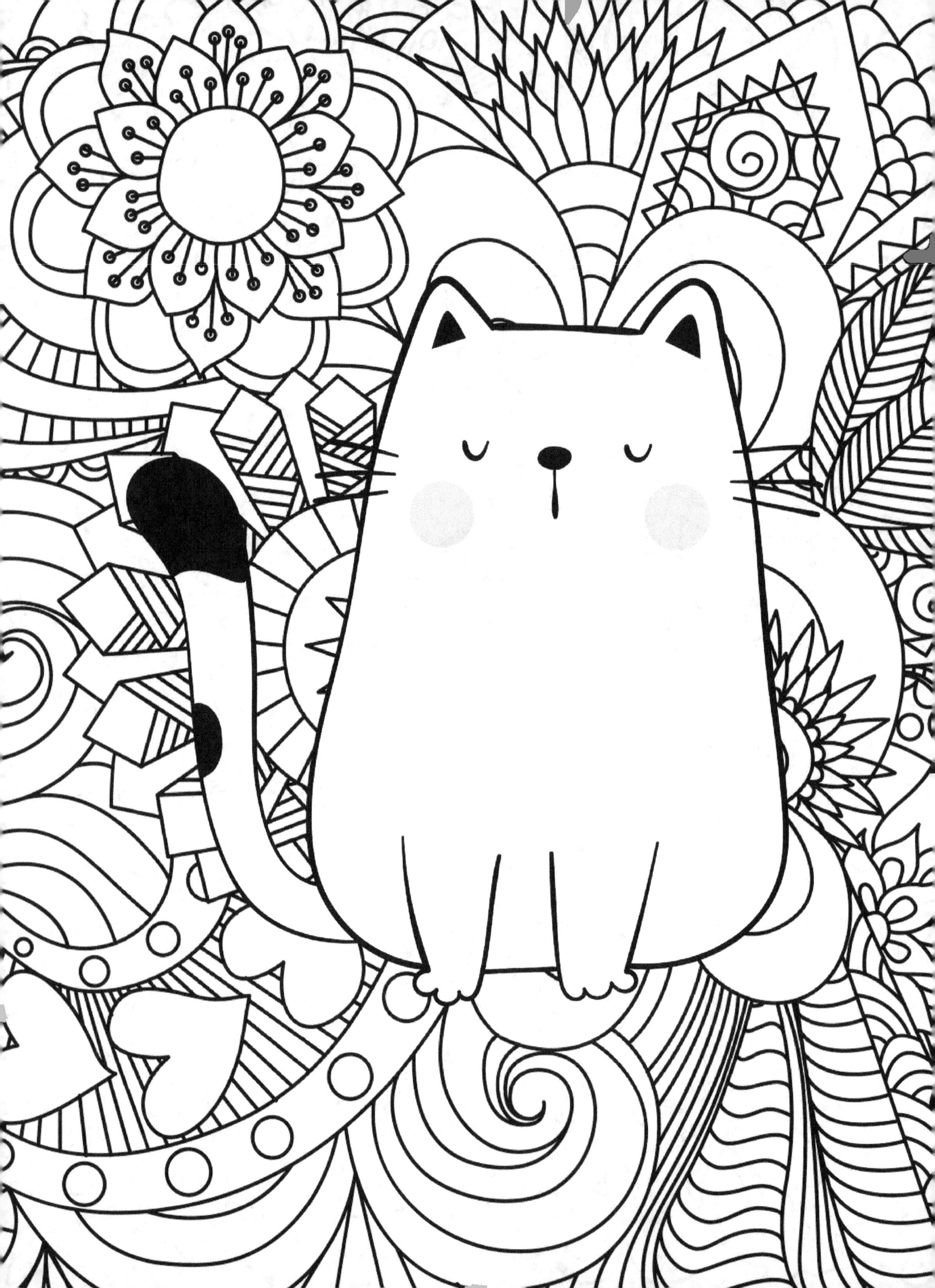

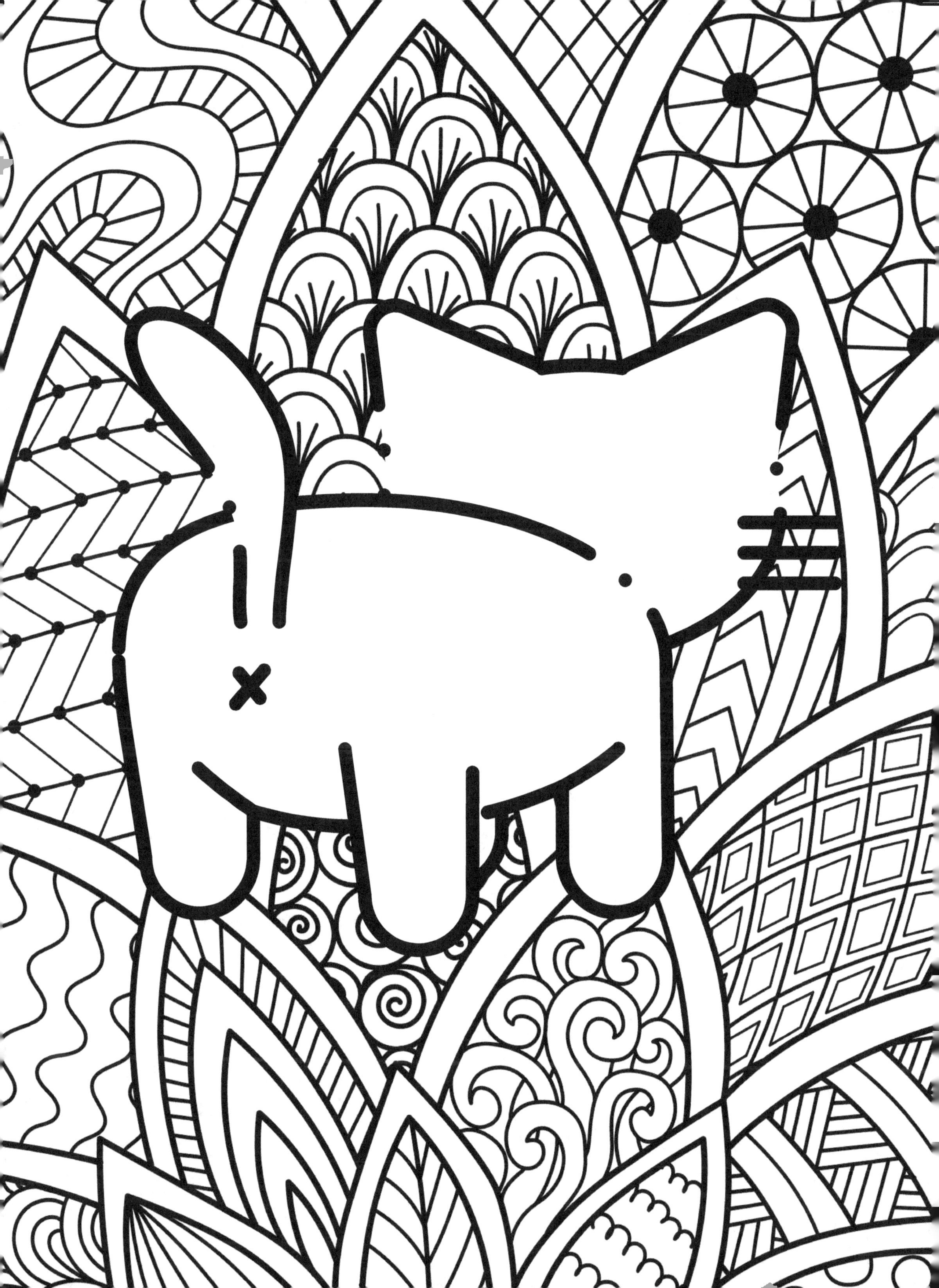

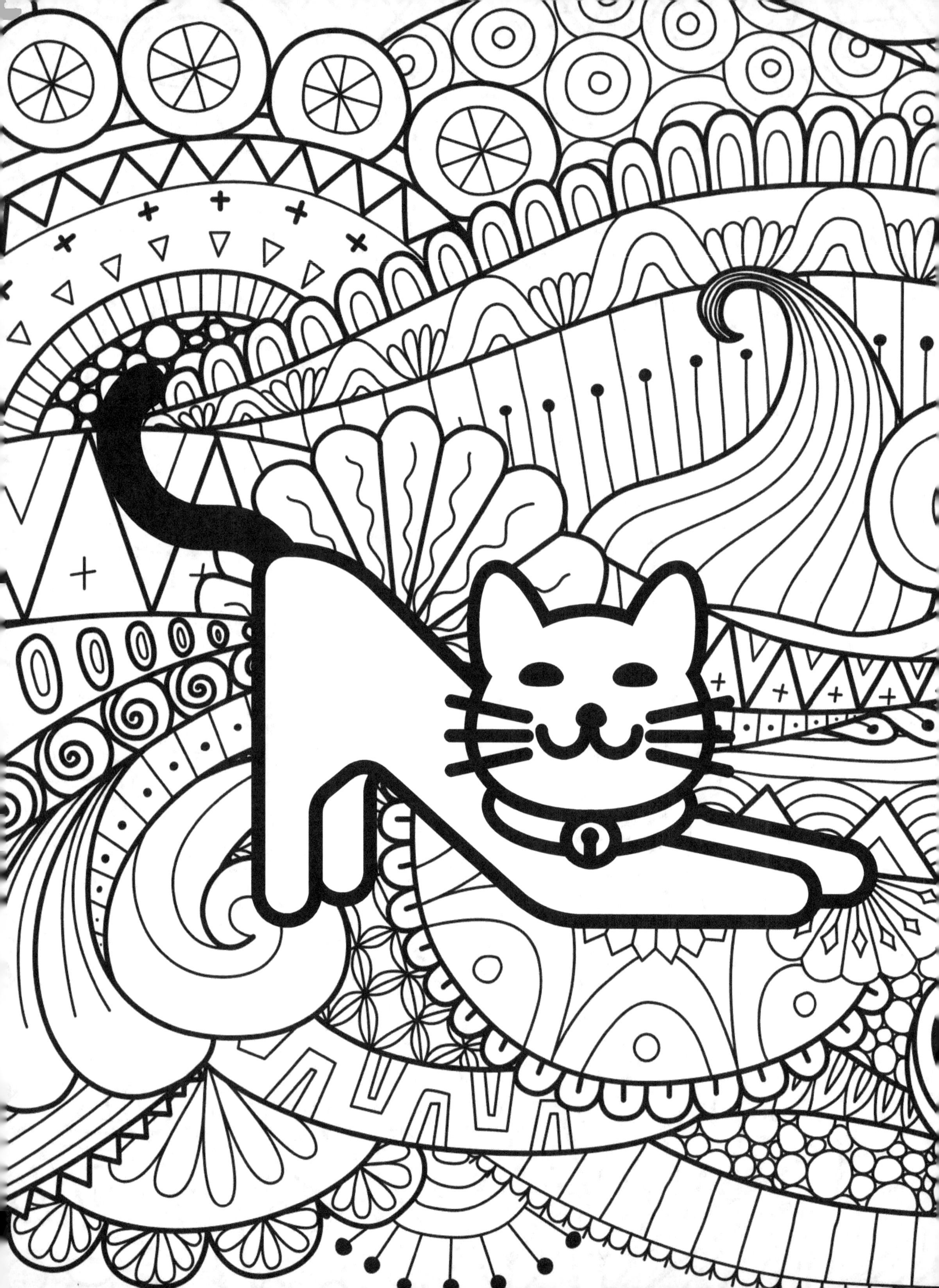

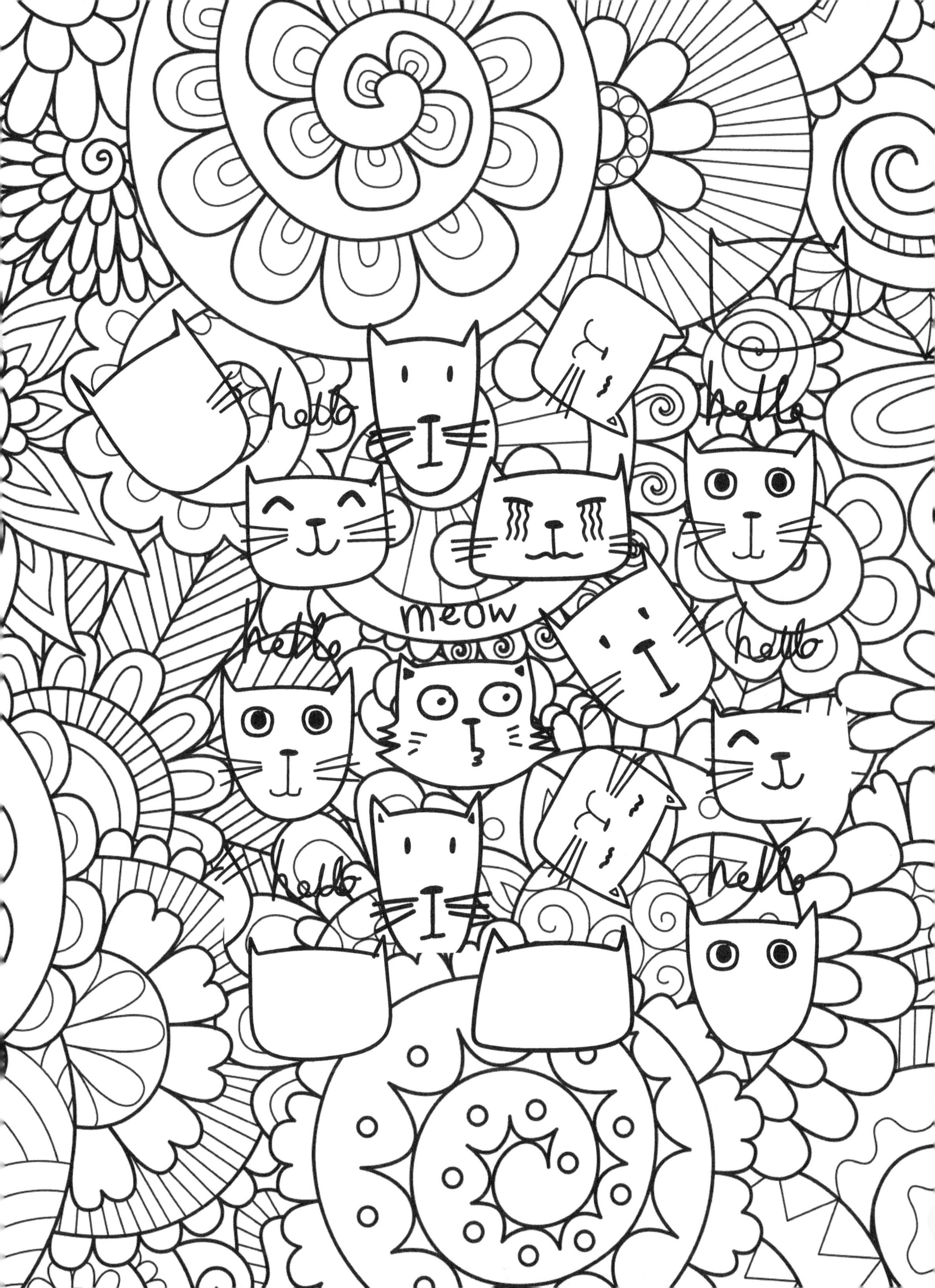

hello
hello
hello
meow
hello
hello

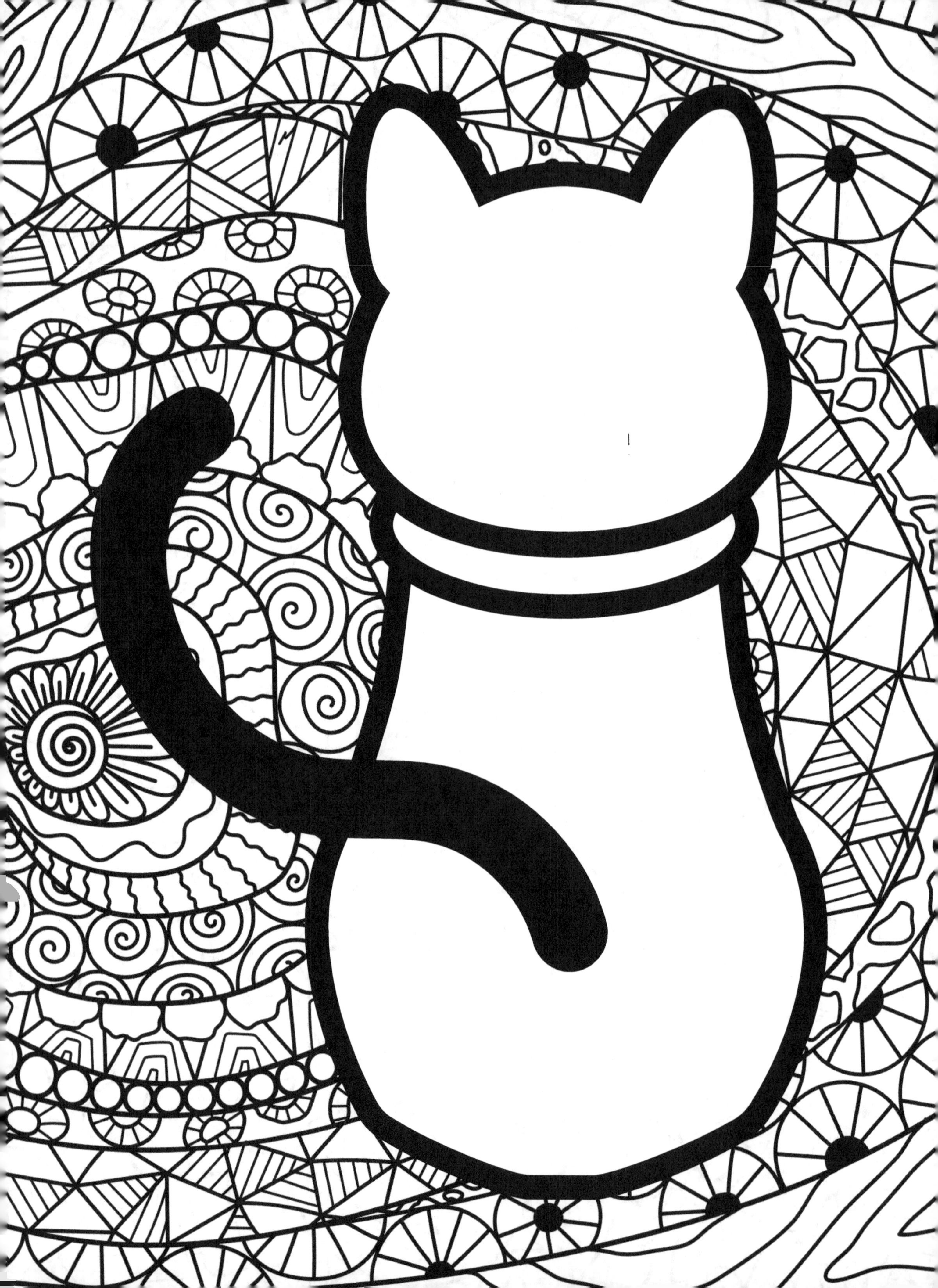

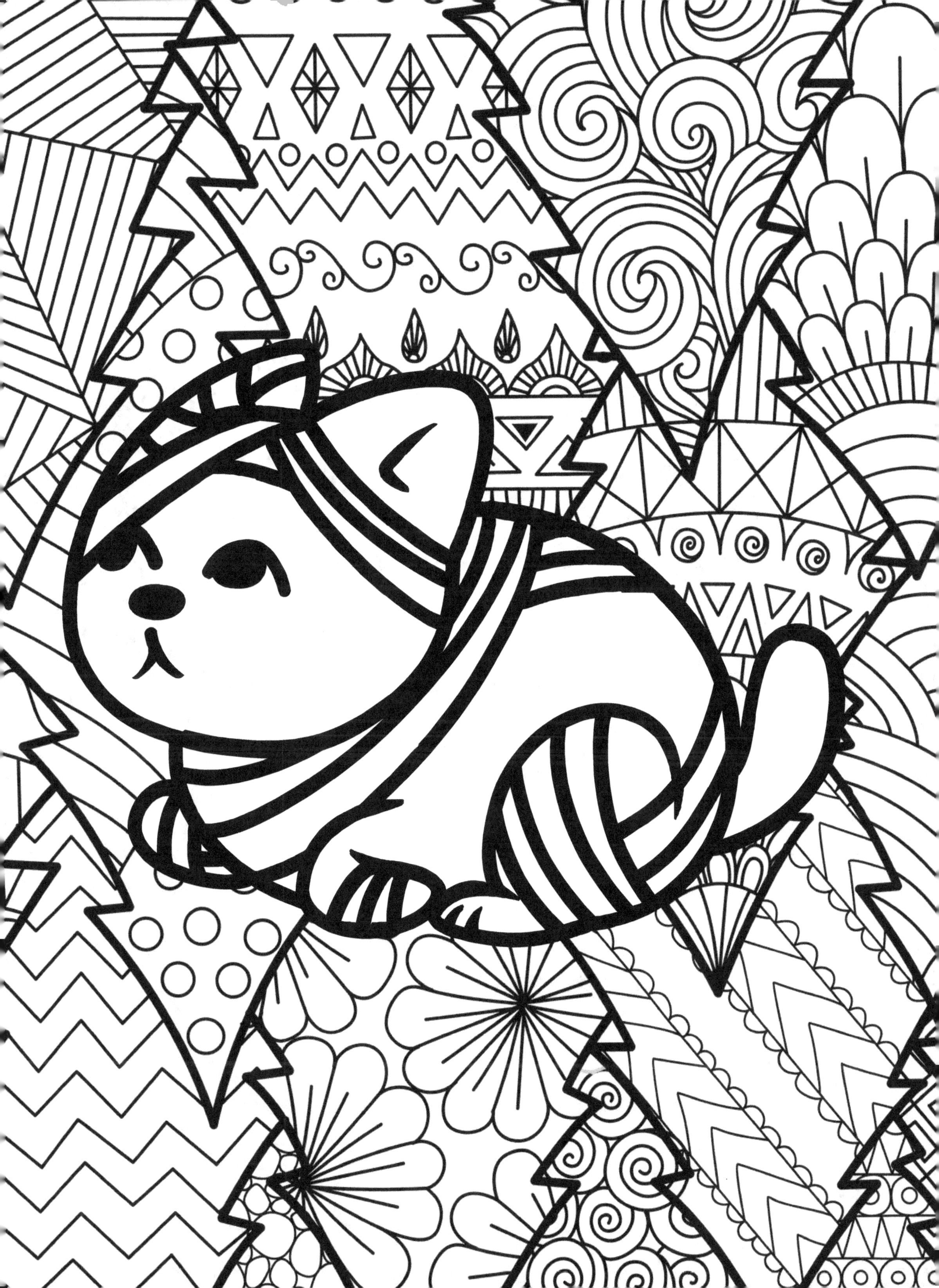

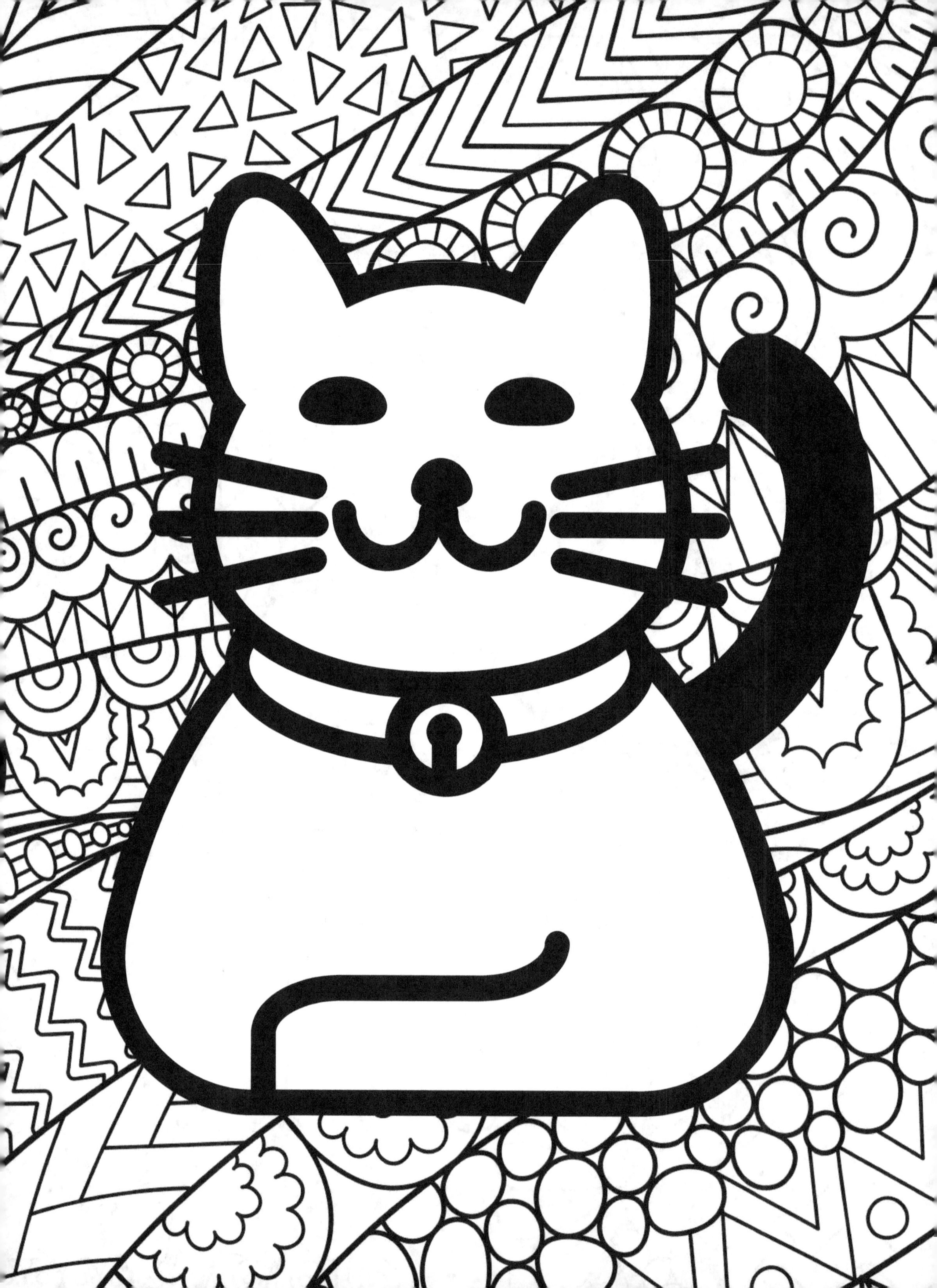

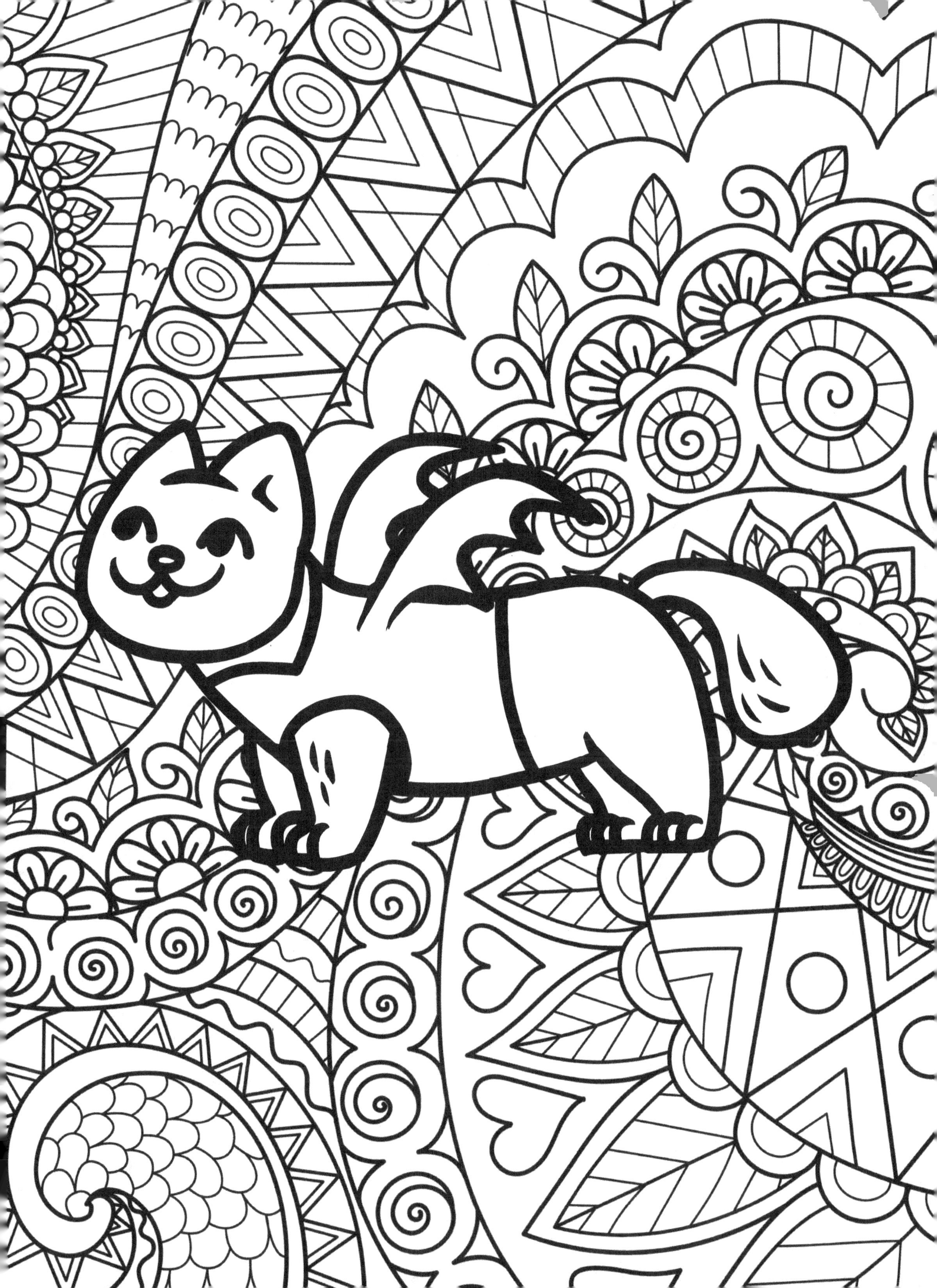

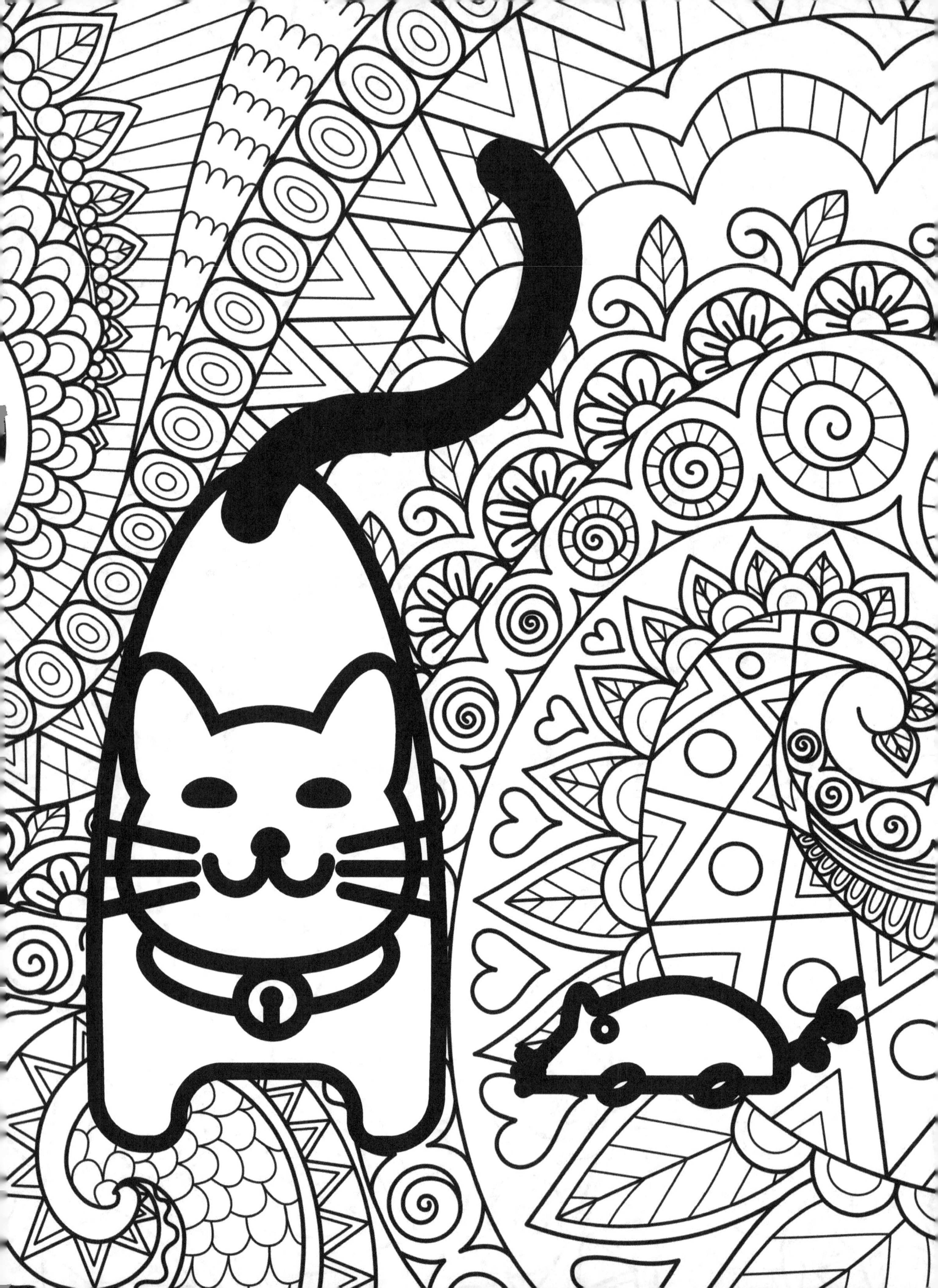

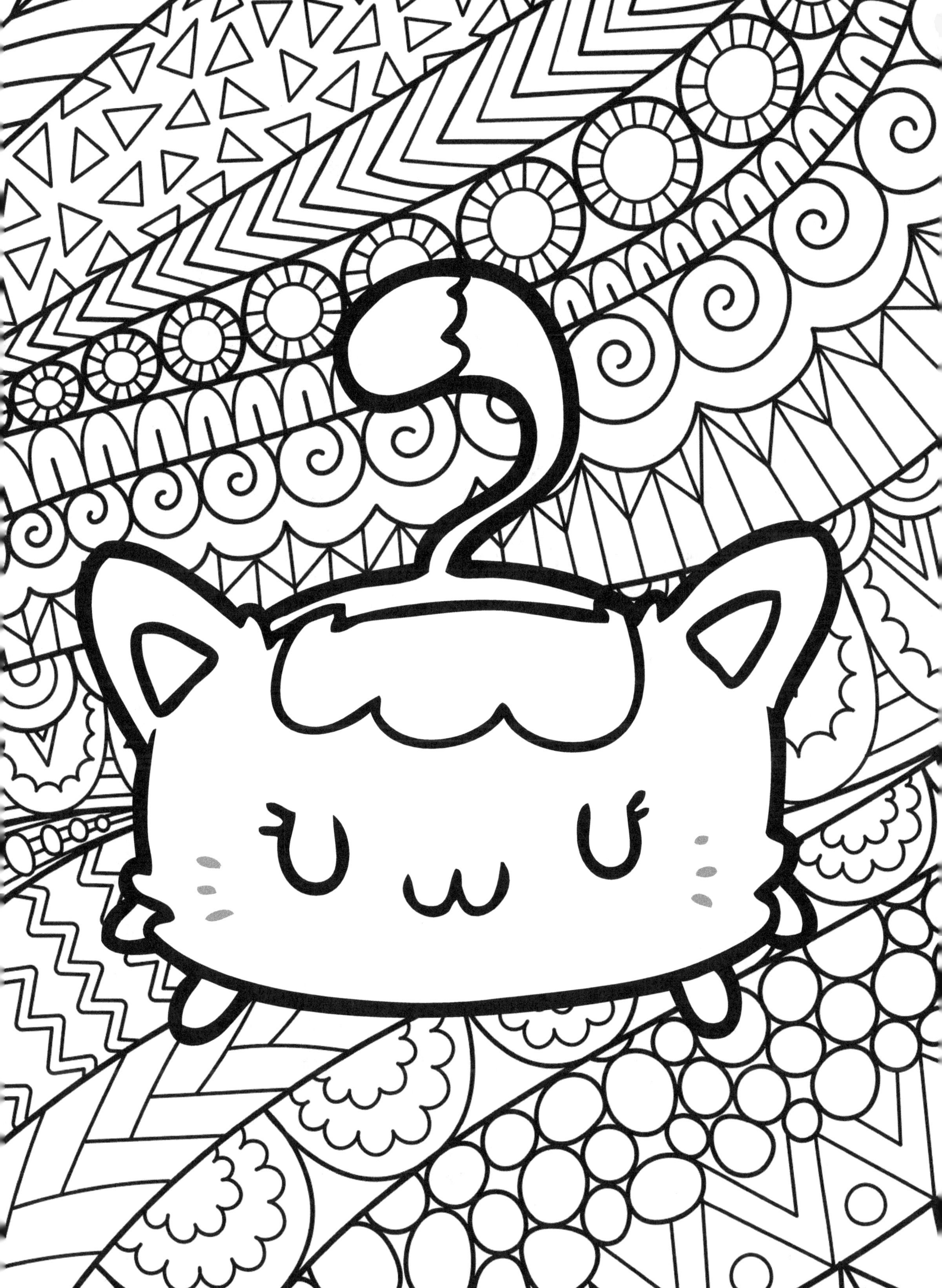

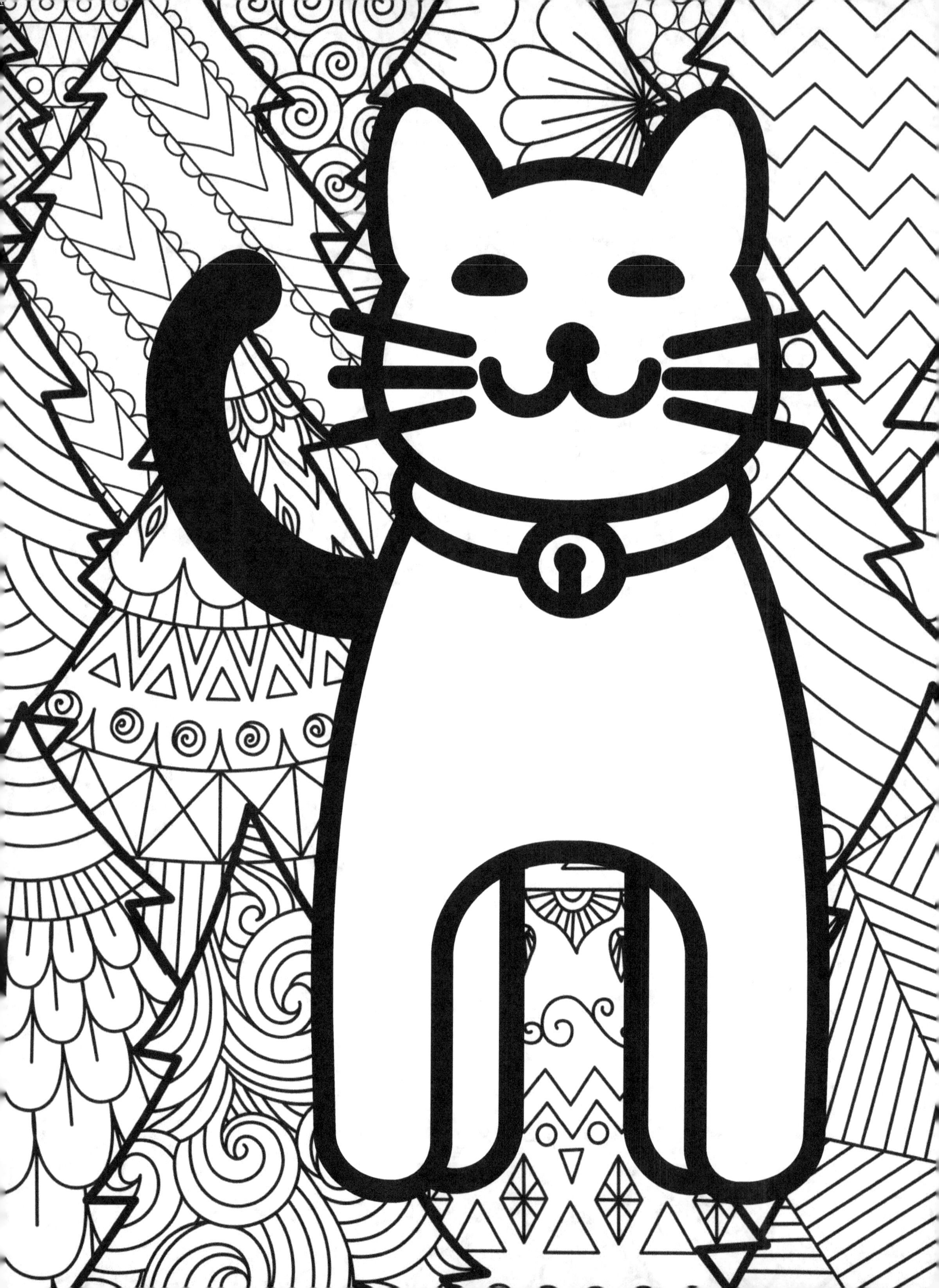

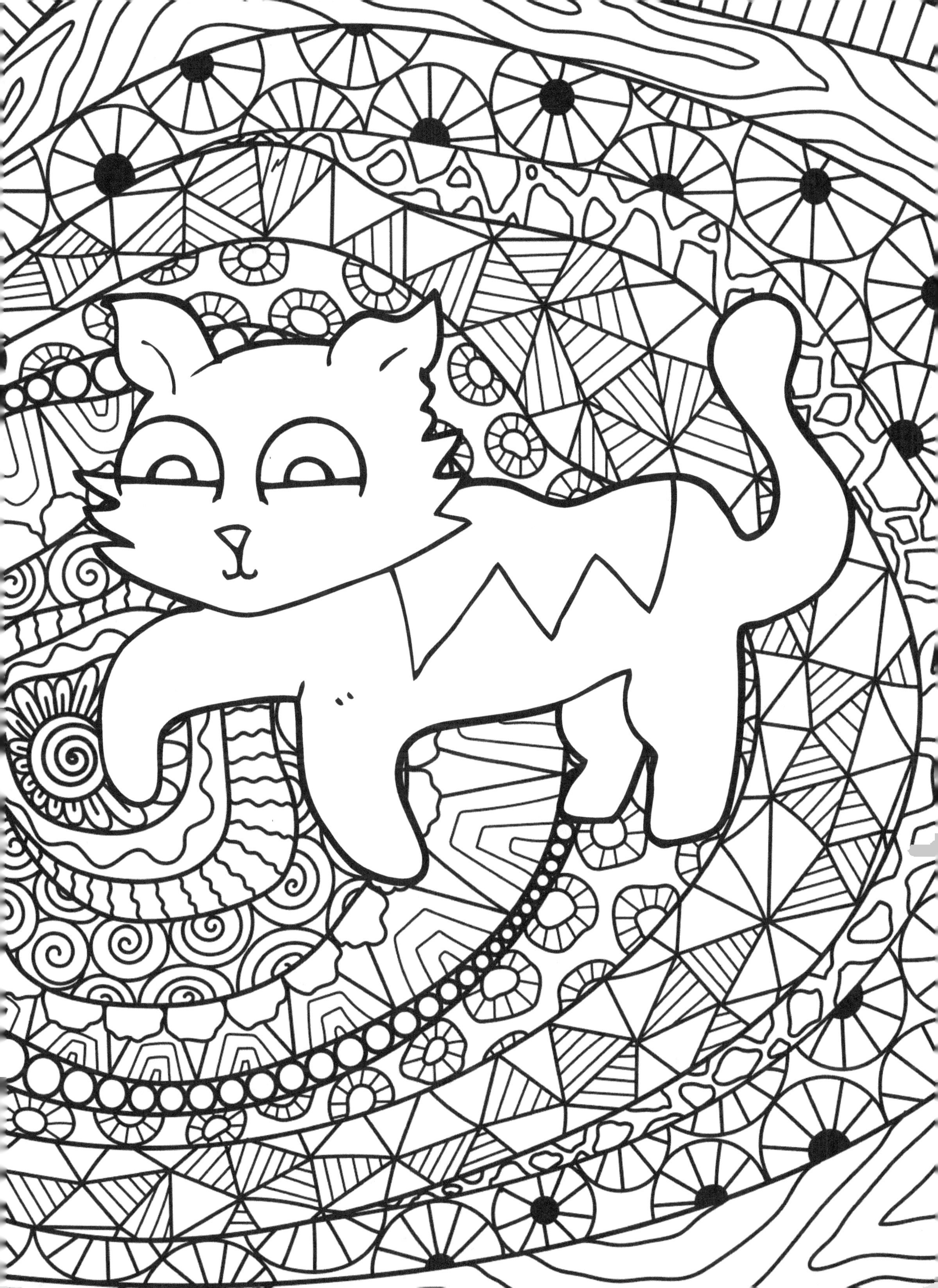

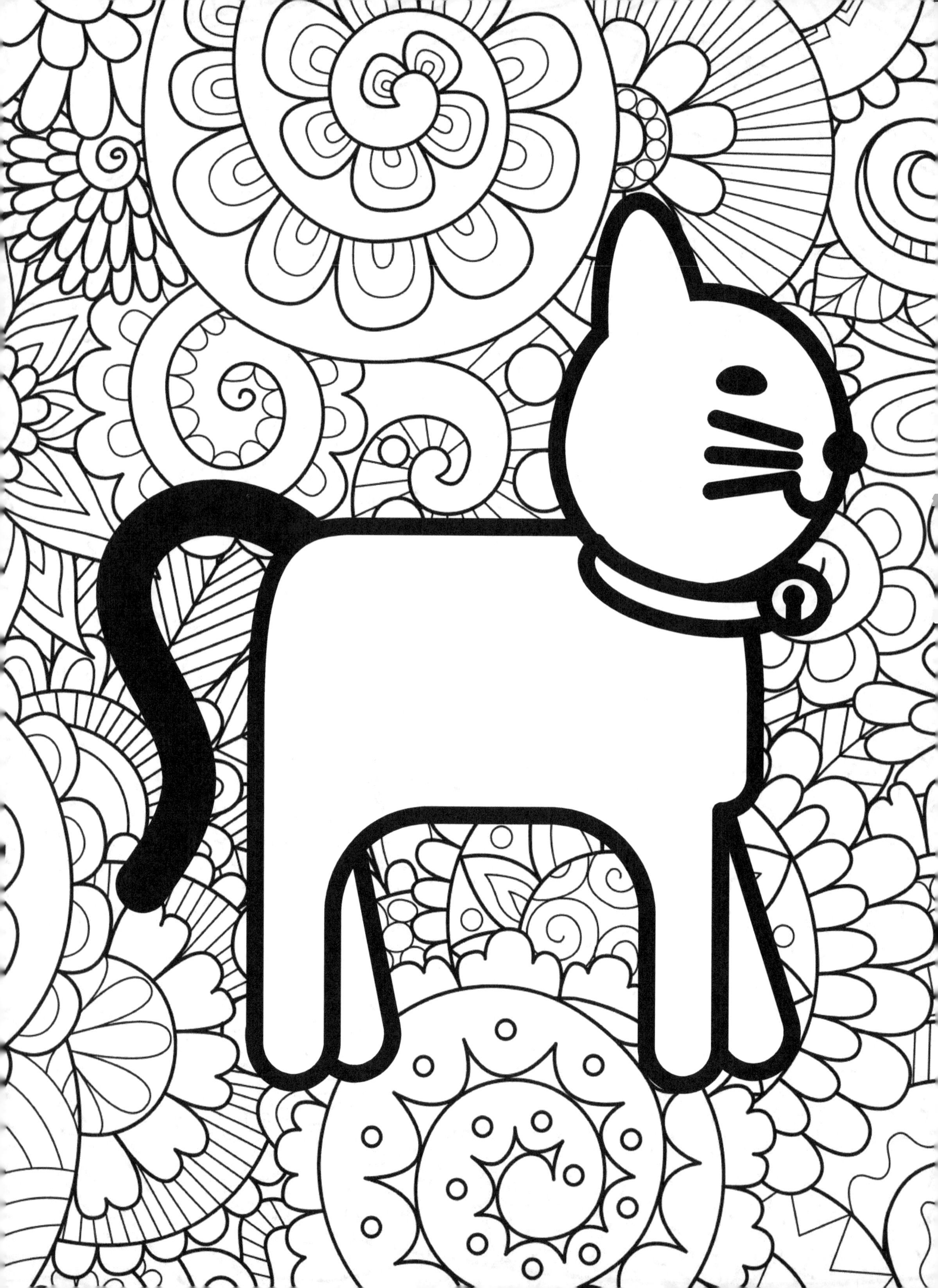

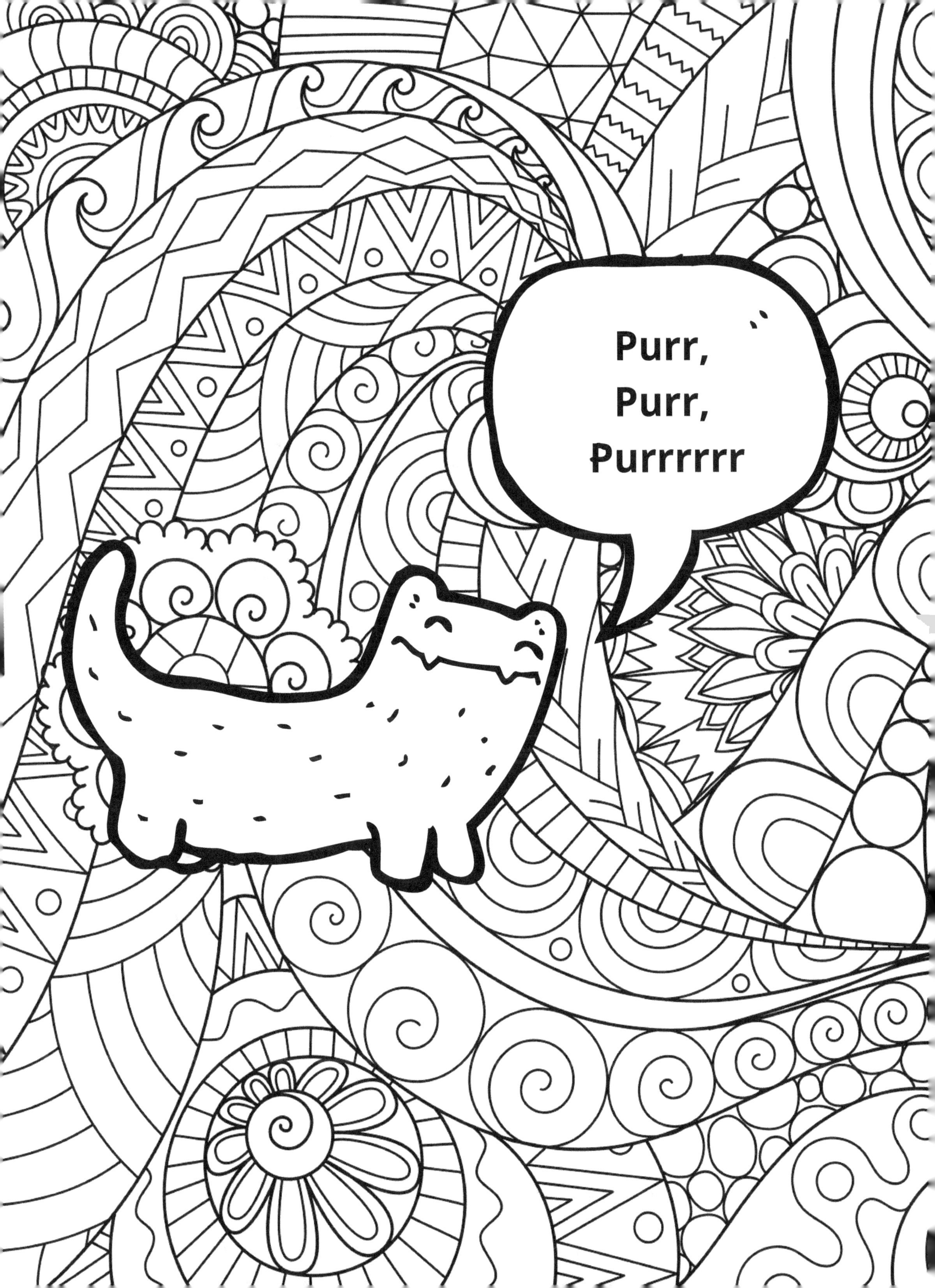

Purr,
Purr,
Purrrrrr

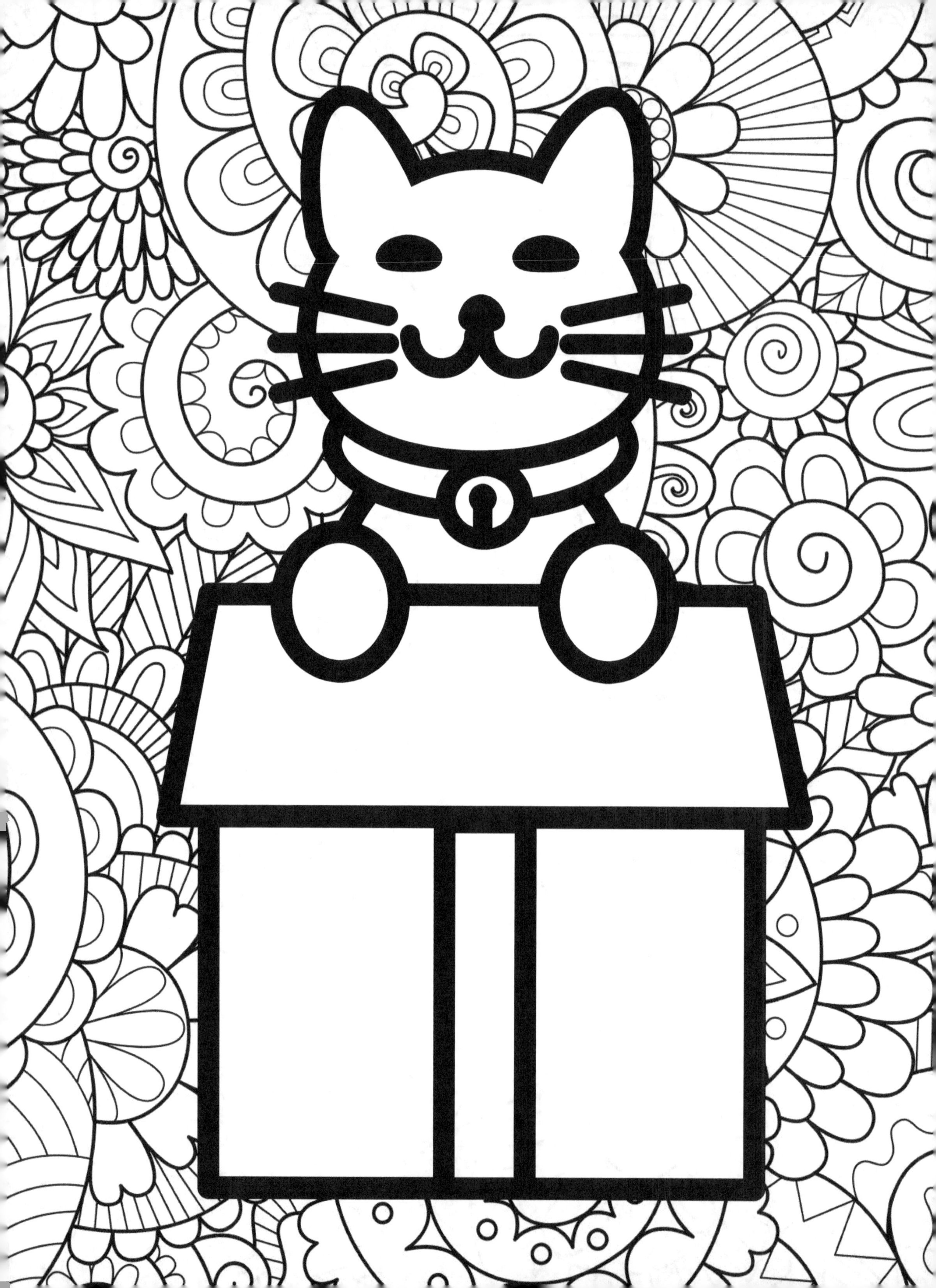

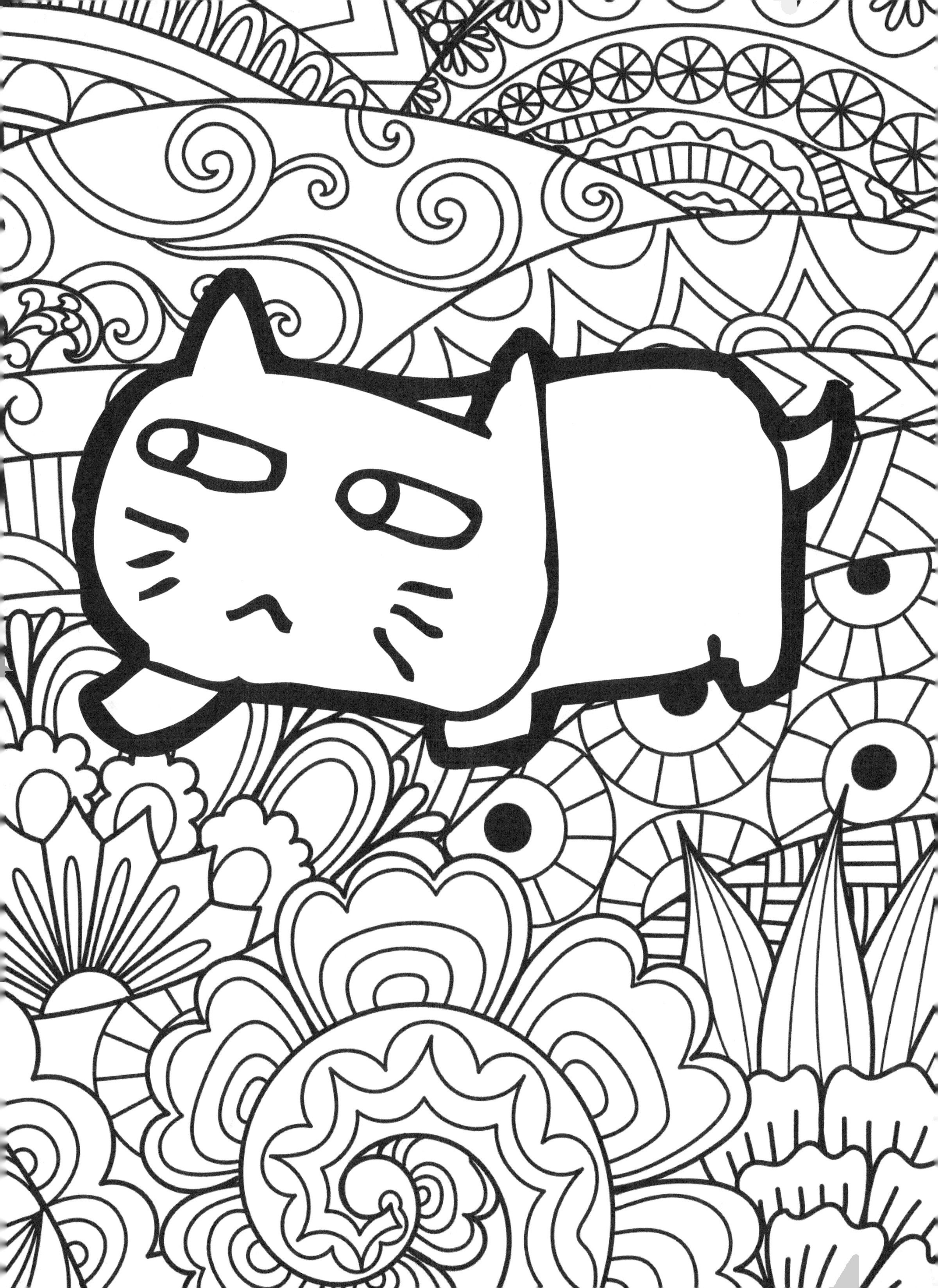

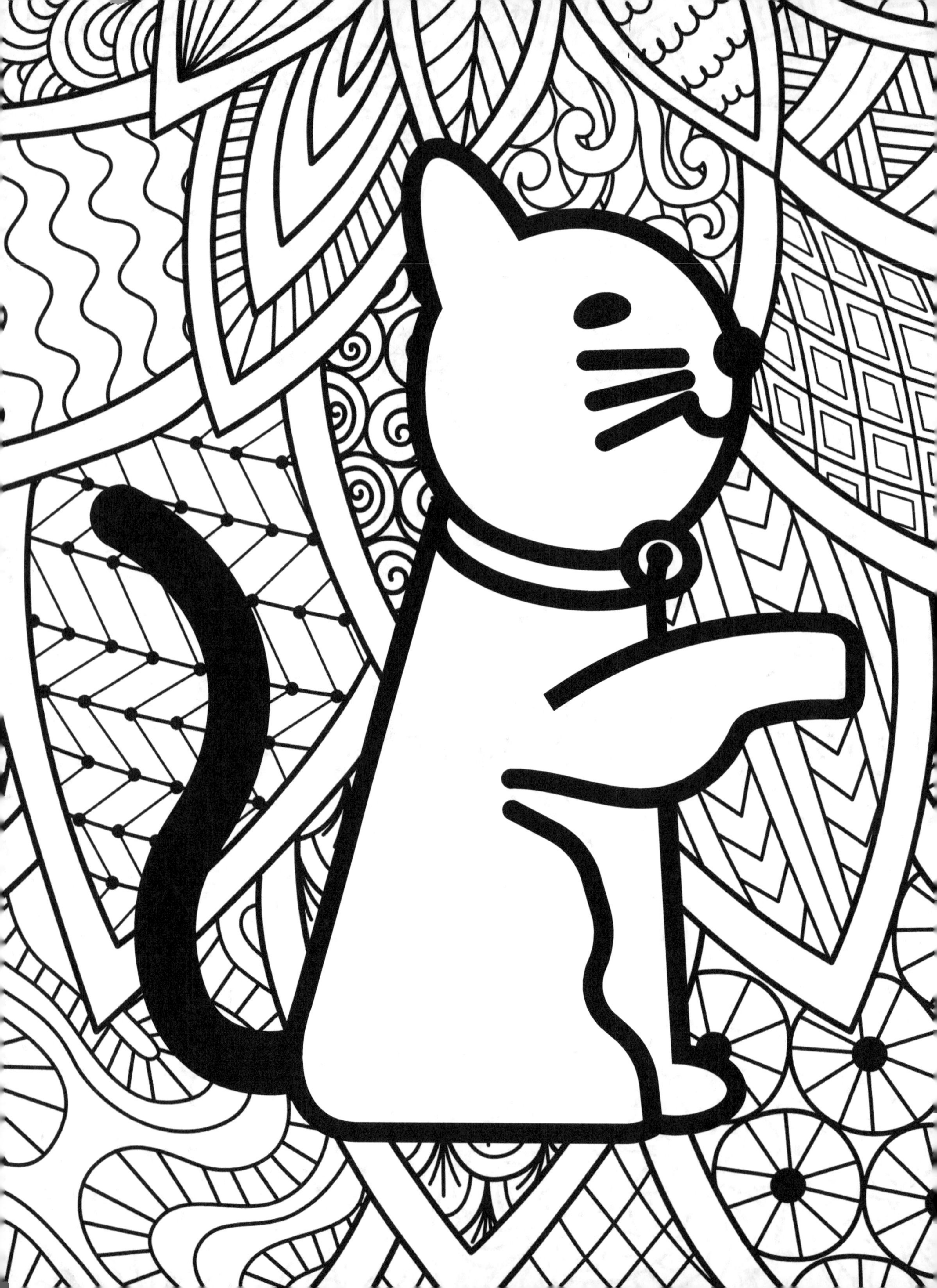

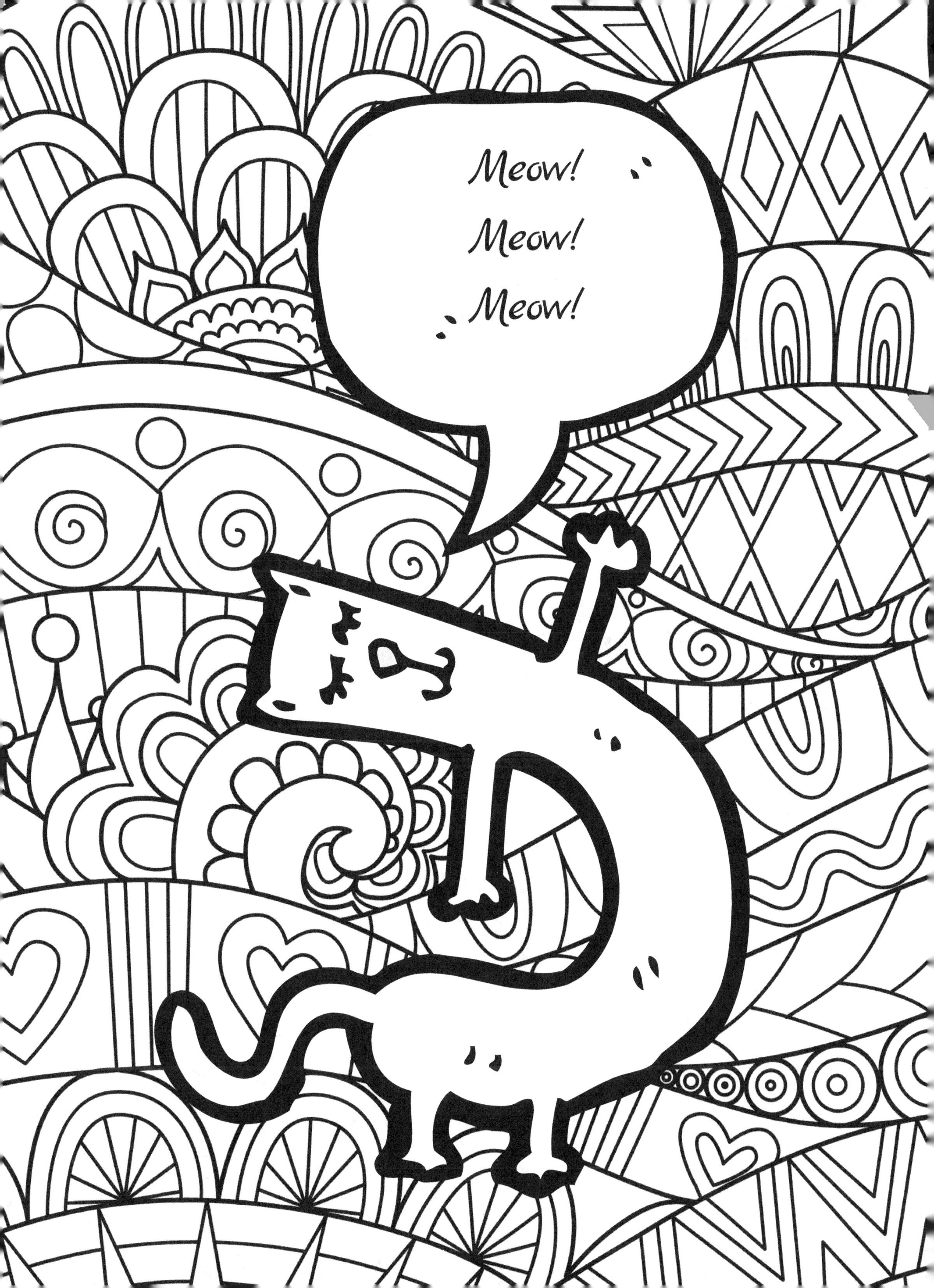

Meow!
Meow!
Meow!

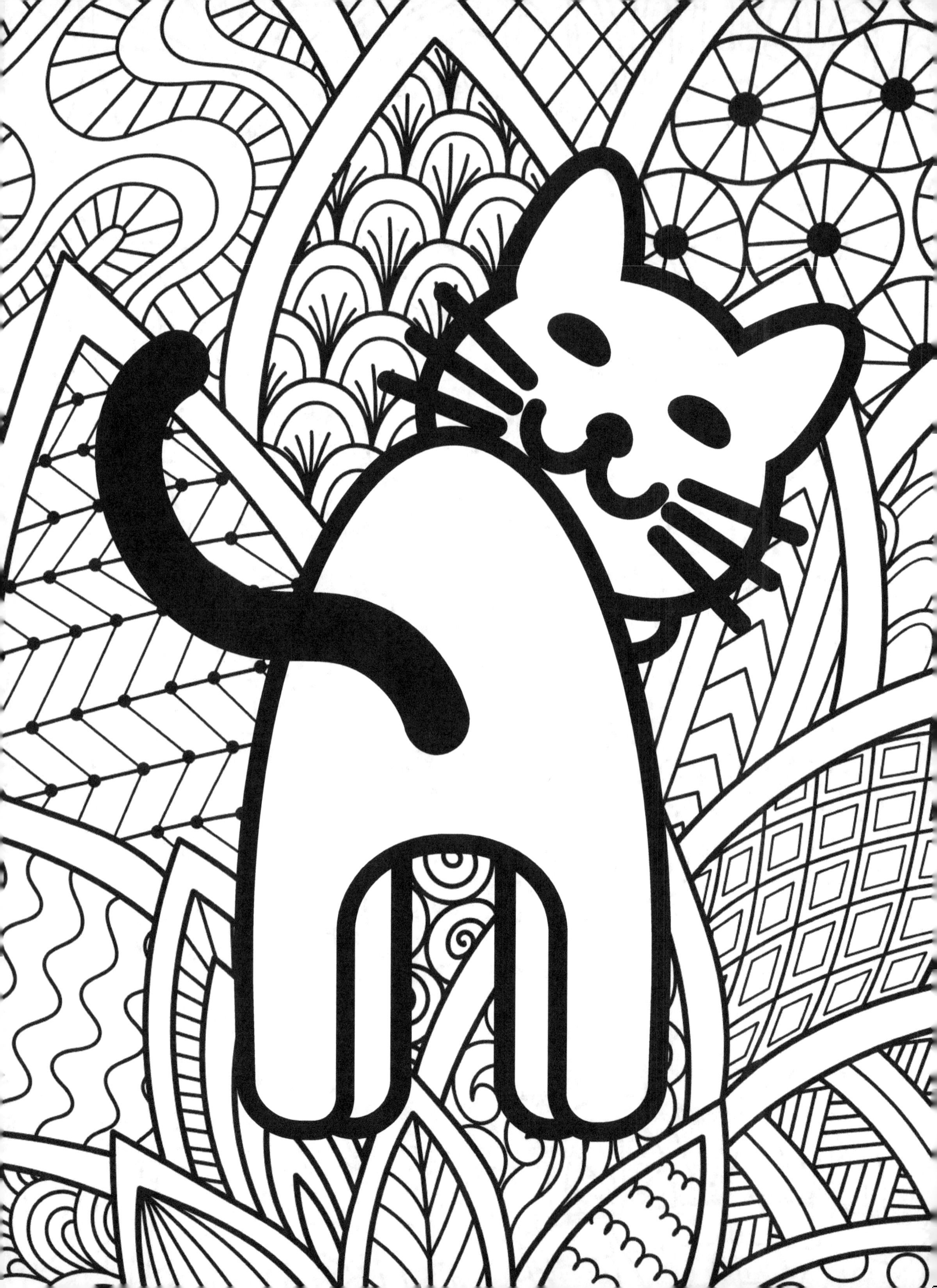

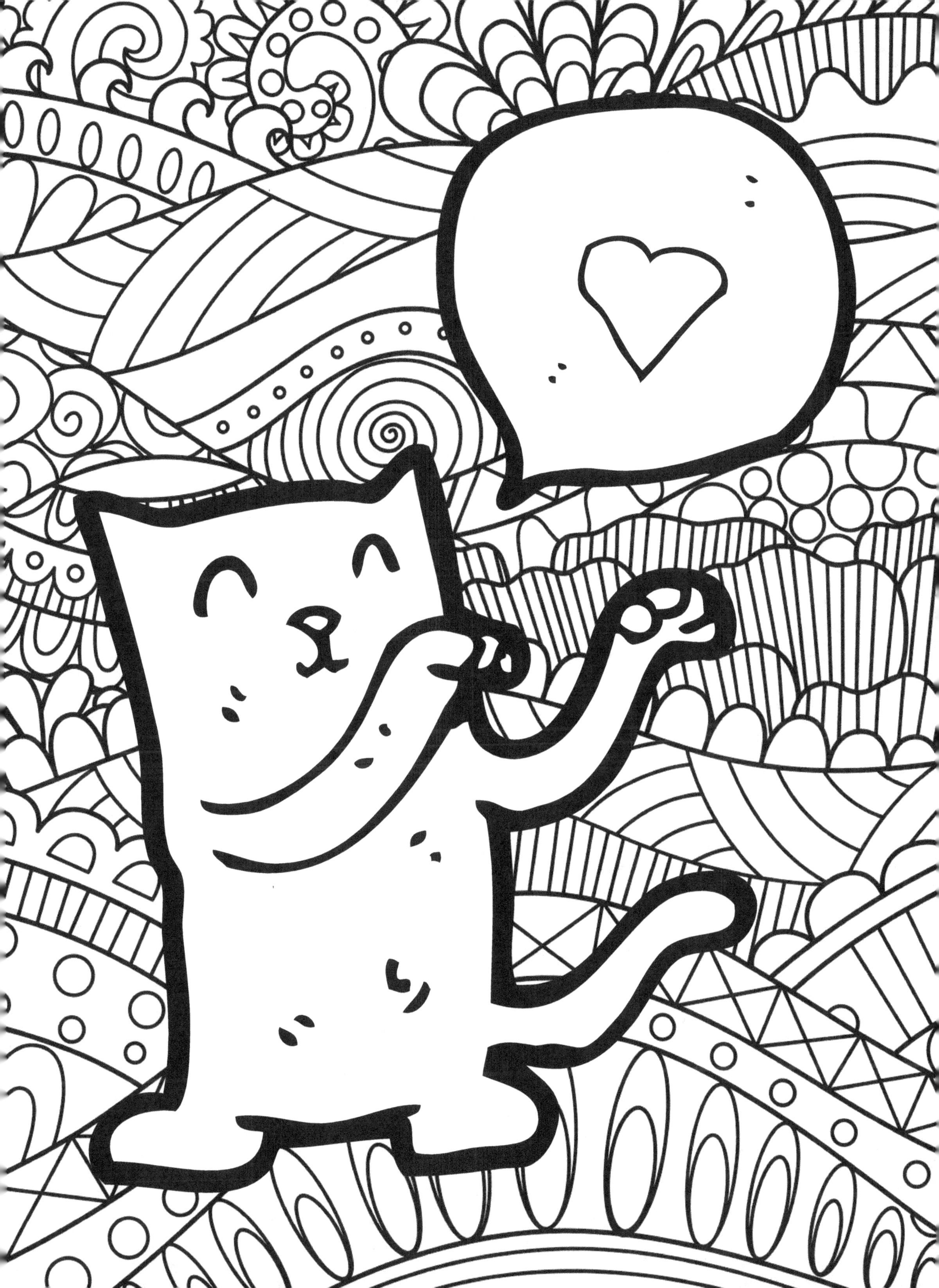

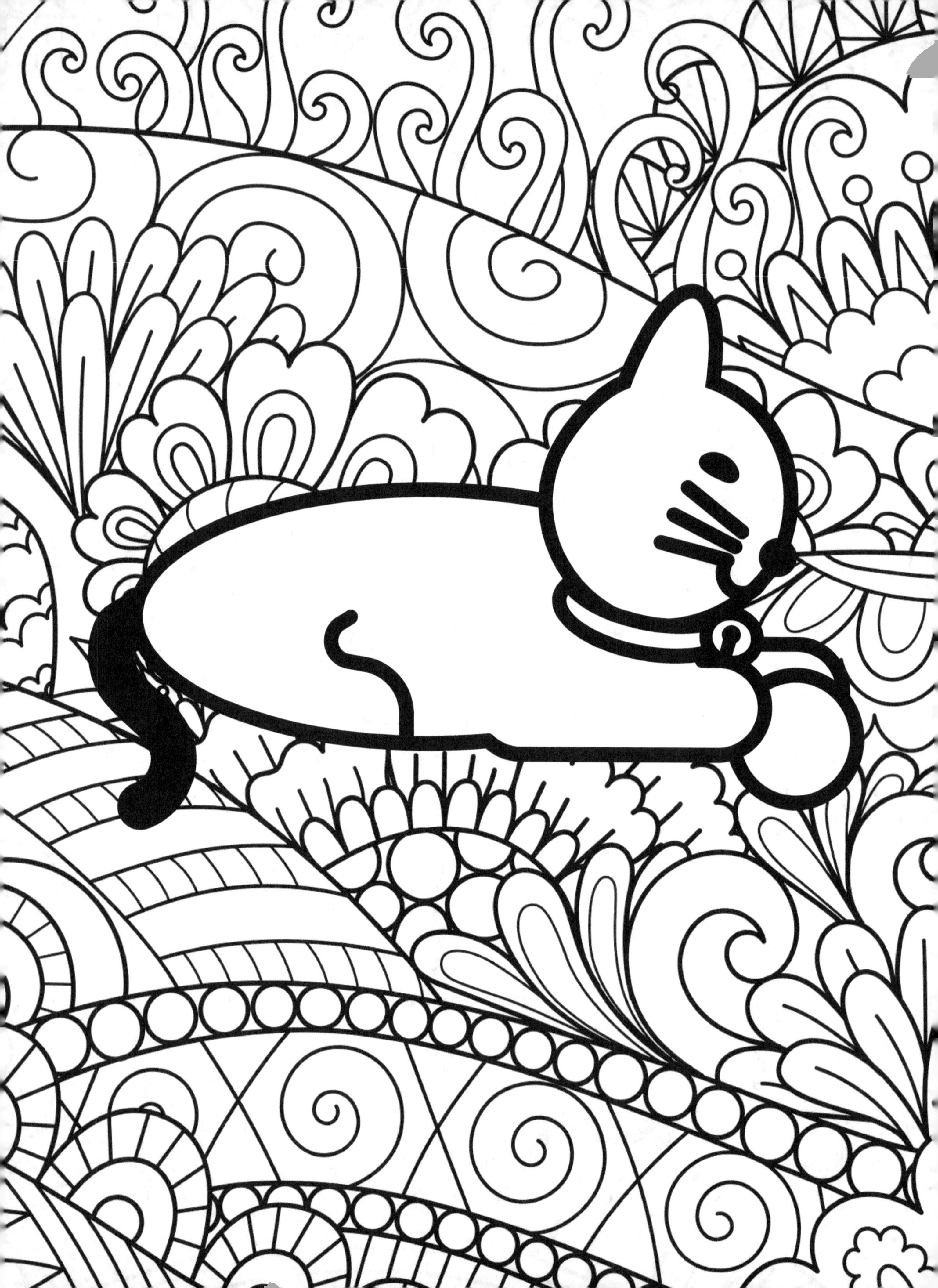

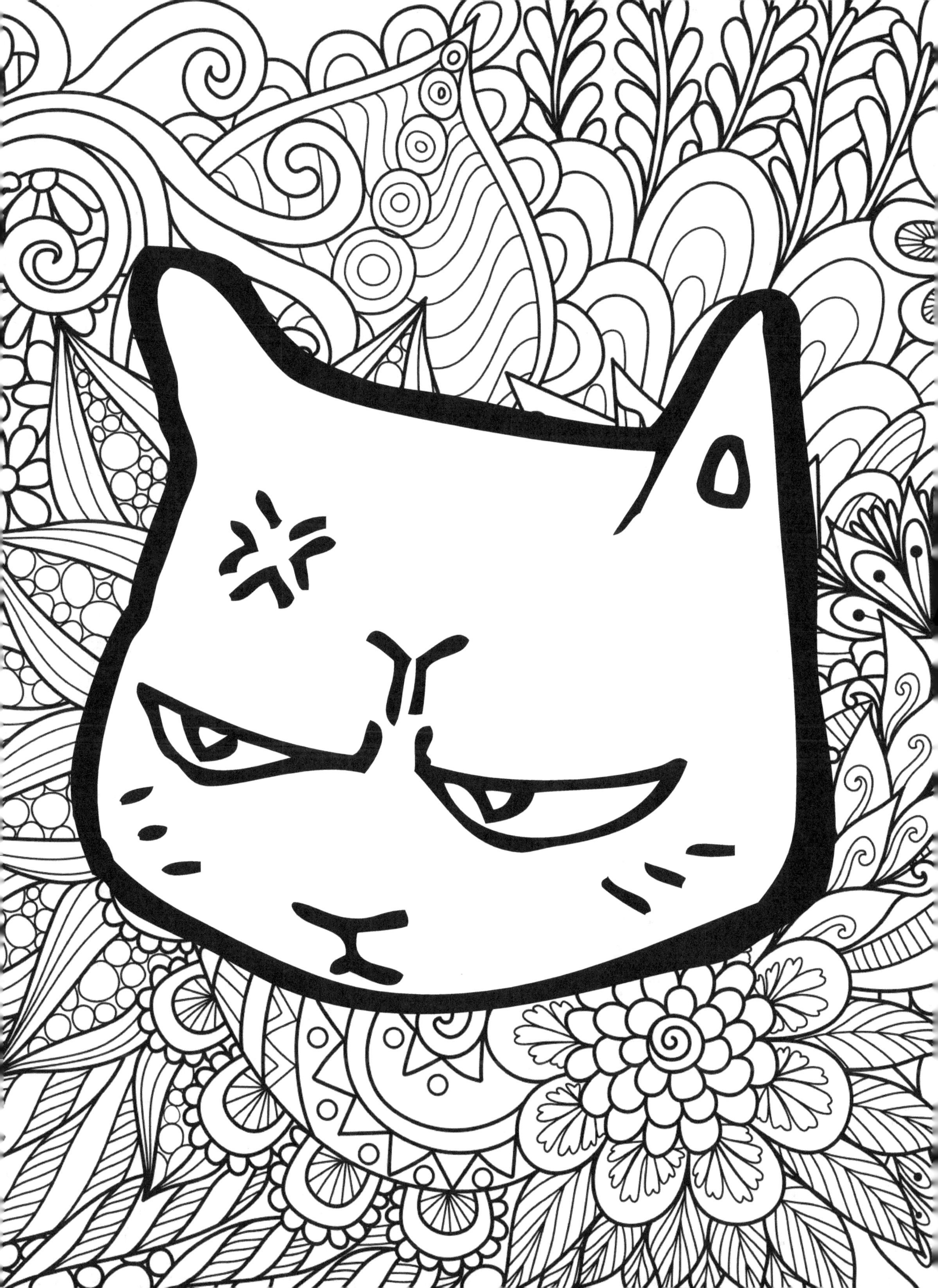

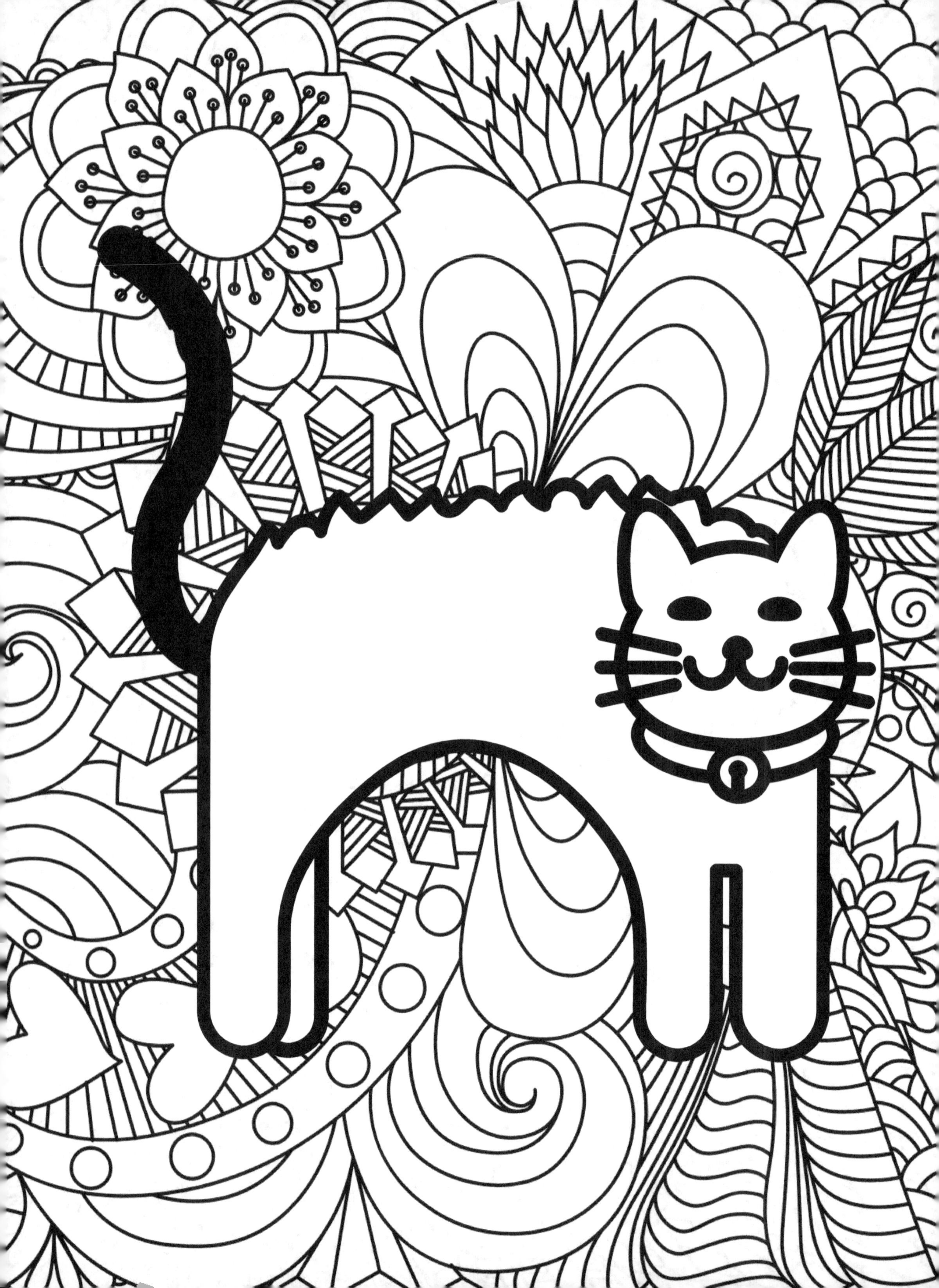

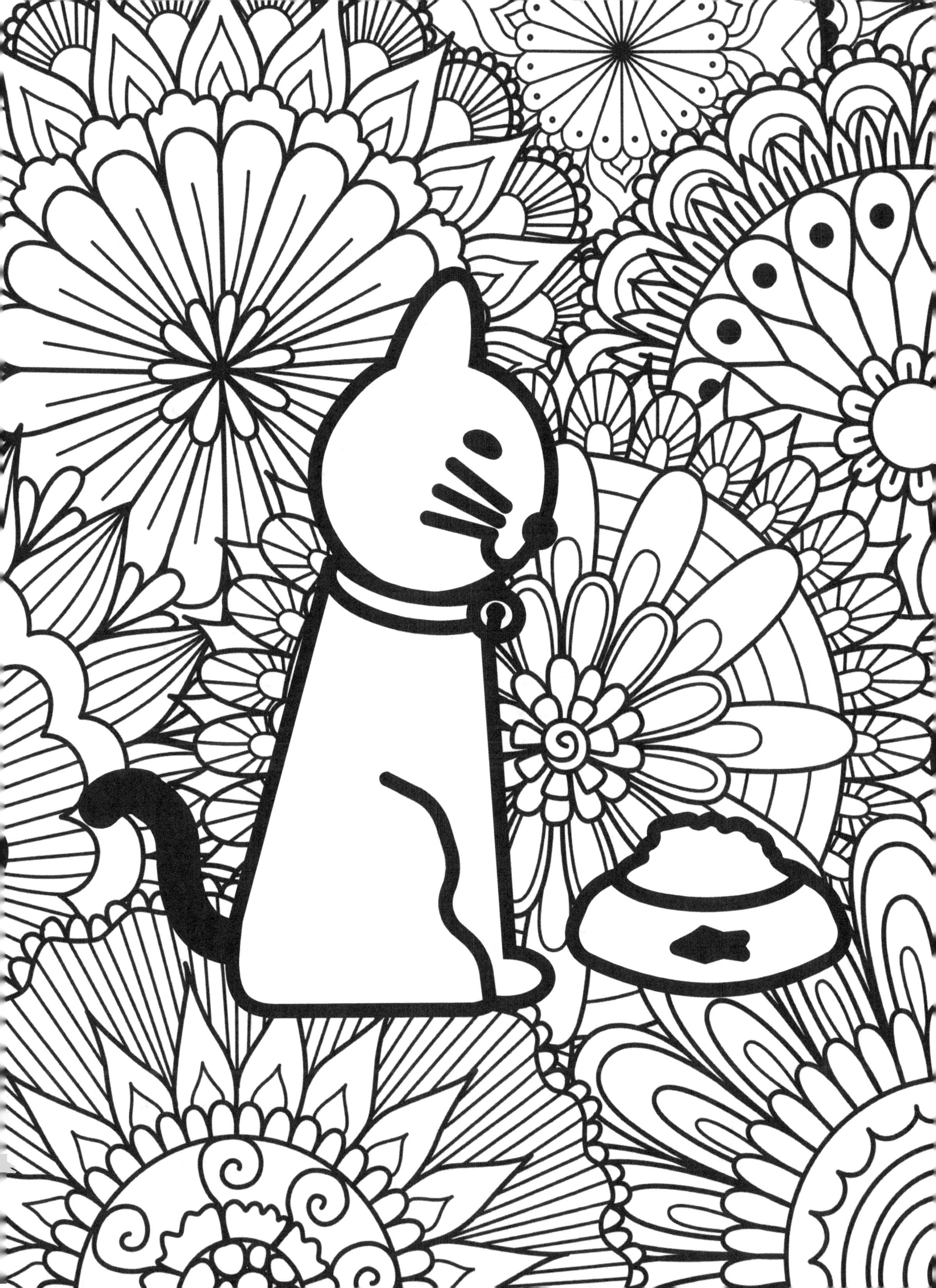

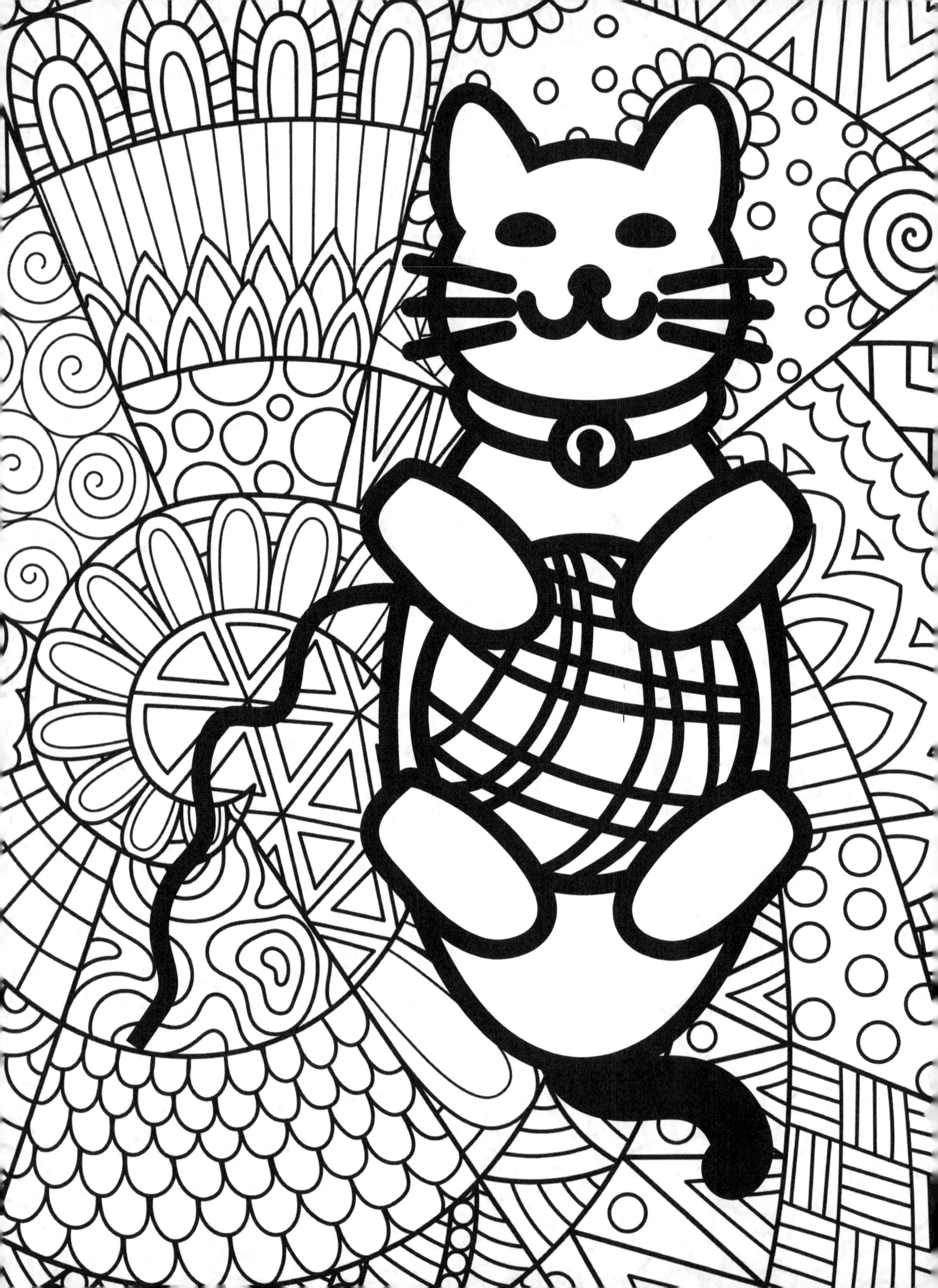

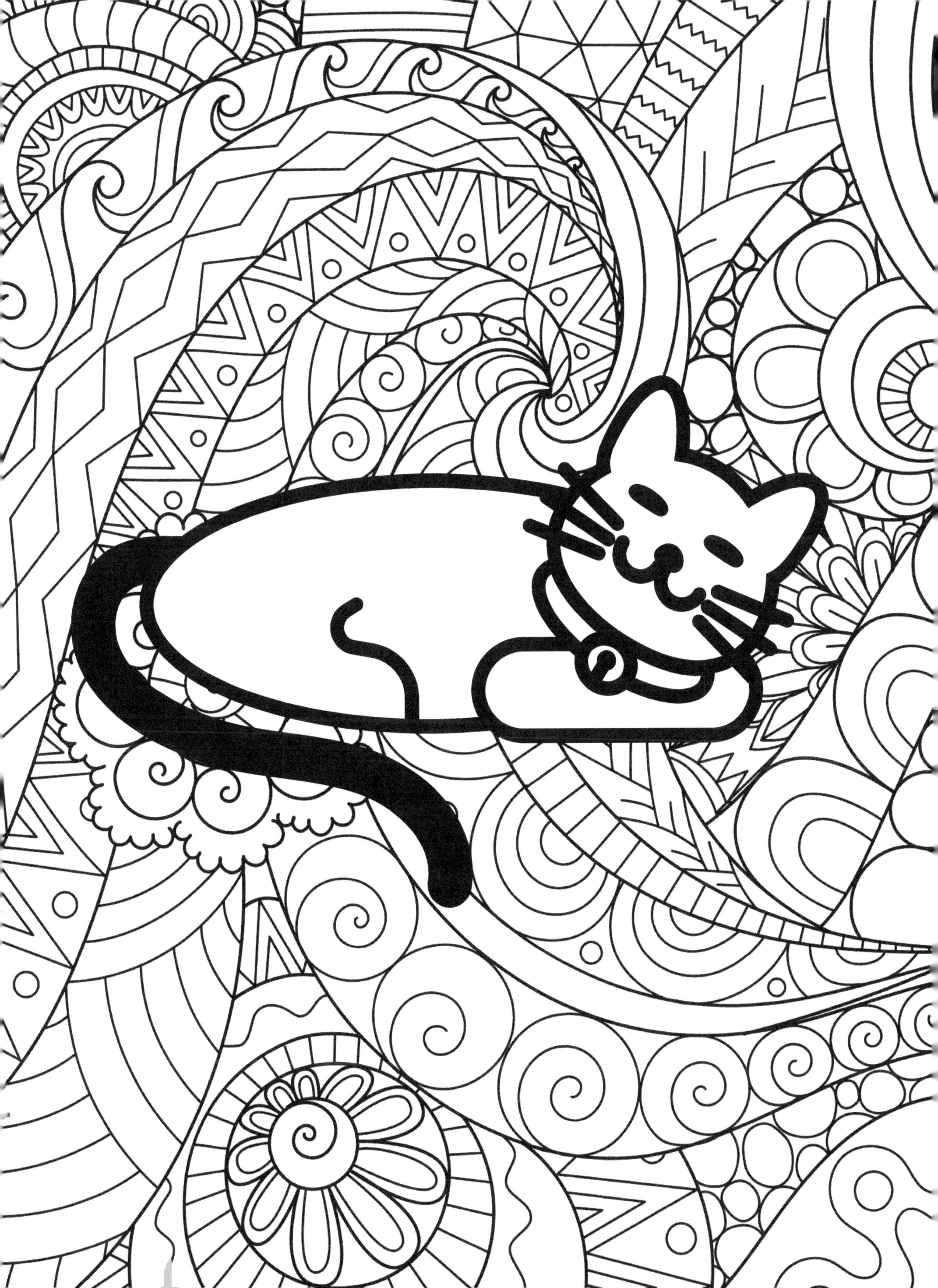

Be on the lookout
for our other
Big Coloring Book
Titles!
Check our author
page on Amazon at:

https://www.amazon.com/Journals-ForYou/e/B08SDWYPJ3